Making Prayer & Meditation Work for You

The Transforming Experience of Practicing Step 11

Includes 90 Daily Meditations

CATHY C.

BALBOA.
PRESS
A DIVISION OF HAY HOUSE

Balboa Press books may be ordered through booksellers or by contacting:

Balboa Press
A Division of Hay House
1663 Liberty Drive
Bloomington, IN 47403
www.balboapress.com
1 (877) 407-4847

Because of the dynamic nature of the Internet, any web addresses or
links contained in this book may have changed since publication and
may no longer be valid. The views expressed in this work are solely those
of the author and do not necessarily reflect the views of the publisher,
and the publisher hereby disclaims any responsibility for them.

The author of this book does not dispense medical advice or prescribe the use
of any technique as a form of treatment for physical, emotional, or medical
problems without the advice of a physician, either directly or indirectly. The
intent of the author is only to offer information of a general nature to help
you in your quest for emotional and spiritual well-being. In the event you use
any of the information in this book for yourself, which is your constitutional
right, the author and the publisher assume no responsibility for your actions.

Any people depicted in stock imagery provided by Thinkstock are
models, and such images are being used for illustrative purposes only.
Certain stock imagery © Thinkstock.

Print information available on the last page.

ISBN: 978-1-5043-5403-5 (sc)
ISBN: 978-1-5043-5404-2 (hc)
ISBN: 978-1-5043-5405-9 (e)

Library of Congress Control Number: 2016904854

Balboa Press rev. date: 5/3/2016

EDITOR'S NOTE

The brief excerpts from the books *Alcoholics Anonymous* and *Twelve Steps and Twelve Traditions* are reprinted with permission of Alcoholics Anonymous World Services, Inc. ("AAWS"). Permission to reprint these excerpts does not mean that AAWS has reviewed or approved the contents of this publication or that AAWS necessarily agrees with the views expressed herein. Additionally, while AA is a spiritual program, AA is not a religious program. Thus, AA is not affiliated or allied with any sect, denomination, or specific religious belief.

Information from *Prayer and Meditation: A Practical Guide to the Life Promised in Step 11* by Tom R., and from his workshops, is used with his permission.

The healing version of the St. Francis Prayer, by Judith Kubish, is used with the author's permission.

This book is based on actual experiences.

Cover design by Craig C.

This book is dedicated to my son, Steven, who is an aspiring author, in the hope that he will never stop believing in himself or in his dreams.

Please know that *there are no limits,* other than those we ourselves assign.

CONTENTS

FOREWORD

For much of my adult life, I have studied the rise and fall of spiritual movements. AA is one such movement, now barely eighty years old. To my surprise, I discovered that many powerful movements were birthed but then lost sight of their original mission and vitality and passed into history. Regarding alcoholics, the Washingtonians were one such movement in the 1800s. Another spiritual group, the Moravians, was amazingly gifted of God with power to change lives, but they vanished after the 1700s.

I believe that today AA stands at a turning point in its own unique history, and we stand here with a chance to make a difference in its future. Will AA continue so that our children and grandchildren may find it if they need to? Or will it become just another movement that passes on to the scrap heap of history? The answer lies within each one of us and will be determined by our willingness to return to our roots: a God-dependent, organic, growing, healthy community. Cathy C. is a brave pioneer, leading the charge for us, calling to anyone who will hear to go back to our roots.

In Dr. Bob and the Good Oldtimers, on page 178, Bill W. is quoted as saying he "always felt something was *lost* from AA when we stopped *emphasizing* morning (prayer and) meditation." That is where much of AA finds itself—lost and disconnected from more than principles. Cathy is part of a movement that seeks to bring back what is vital and missing. In this magnificent personal work of Cathy's, she emphasizes again for us this most important fact and gives us a well-lit path to follow. She has cut away the vines and bushes that have overgrown the path and cleared the way for all of us to follow—and write our own story, in the process.

For anyone just beginning this exciting adventure, you'll soon discover that you couldn't ask for a better guide than Cathy C.'s book, *Making Prayer and Meditation Work for You.* Cathy does not reveal theory here but her own precious and personal experience. As much as anyone I know, Cathy took the principles she learned—all true to AA literature and history—and has woven a garment of experience: warm and inviting, inspiring and contagious.

Cathy's book is straightforward and easy to understand and follow. If you are just starting to meditate or are looking for someone's revealing and personal practice to guide you, you have found the right book! After fourteen years of searching, in AA she discovered these basic, foundational principles. And she treats them with great honor and respect, for they are what truly matter most in recovery: the restoration of what the steps were intended to do, which is to bring us to an intimate relationship with the God of the steps. She does this, and she does it very well. This book is solidly spiritual and entirely practical.

Many people in recovery come to experience God but have difficulty articulating it. Cathy both experiences God and communicates with great clarity and giftedness. Her honesty is disarming; after reading her book, you may feel like you have been friends forever. She opens her heart and shares her journey into this most desirable of relationships, the one which she has developed with God.

Others who have some initial spiritual experience are lost when it comes to knowing how to grow it, how to enlarge it. Bill W. said that AA is a sort of spiritual kindergarten: we need to begin here and nurture this relationship, so our roots go down deep, and then reach up wide to the world around us. We look around for help, for guides, and we see our friends as lost as we are. We then wonder what is wrong. We may discover truth about our condition in what Bill W. wrote in a 1958 *Grapevine* article.

> Sometimes, when friends tell us how well we are doing, we know better inside. We know we aren't doing well enough. We still can't handle life, as life is. There must be a serious flaw somewhere in our spiritual practice and development. What then is it? The chances are better than even that we shall locate our trouble in our … neglect of AA's Step 11—prayer, meditation, and the guidance of God. The other steps can keep most of us sober and somehow functioning. But Step 11 can keep us growing, if we try hard and work at it continually.

Cathy's groundbreaking book shows us the way out of this dilemma.

Each one of us is called to a certain destiny to do the work of God. We are told, "We are in the world to play the role He assigns."[1] Without an encounter with this God, how are we to find our place in this world? AA number 3 tells us, on page 158 of the "Big Book" *Alcoholics Anonymous,* "He had found God—and in finding God had found himself." This is the journey each one of us must be on, if we are to discover not only the meaning of life but also the meaning of my life, of your life.

My prayer for you, as you open this living document, is that you lay aside any prejudice you may have and open your mind to having a new experience with God. If you do, you will. It's a promise. Let Cathy be your trustworthy guide. She is a courageous woman who has overcome great personal tragedy to discover a new world. She has discovered the God of AA to be easily accessible, passionate about her, and always near, always within reach. She's authentic and the living, breathing embodiment of what Step 11 means.

I'm happy to endorse Cathy's book and give it my full recommendation for those who are exploring spiritual growth.

May we join with other AAs who said in former times that "the central fact of our lives today is the absolute certainty that our Creator has entered into our hearts and lives in a way which is indeed miraculous."[2]

—Tom R.

PREFACE

The benefits of meditation have been widely researched and accepted by members of both spiritual organizations and the scientific/medical community for years.

I had tried to learn how to meditate for over thirty years with Transcendental meditation, Buddhist meditation, Yoga meditation, etc. I could never accomplish the first step that they all required: a quiet mind. I had given up.

Then, in November of 2010, I was invited to attend a weekend prayer and meditation retreat that was associated with Twelve Step recovery programs. This was the first time I had ever heard of an in-depth discussion of Step 11: prayer and meditation. I agreed to go, without any real expectation of getting much out of the retreat. But Tom R., the leader of the retreat, gave me tools that made meditation work for me.

Using Tom's technique, I went from not being able to meditate to enjoying a practice of daily meditation that has continued for years. I rarely miss a day, because I enjoy it so much and have found it to be so beneficial.

Our Twelve Step literature includes this description of meditation. "It is essentially an *individual adventure,* something which each one of us works out in his own way."[3]

Tom R. opened the door for me to the most exciting adventure I have ever undertaken! The workable approach to meditation outlined in this book can help you develop and enjoy consistent two-way communications with God.

I will explain the focused meditation technique, outline some suggested meditations, and describe how I have applied what I was taught to develop my own meditation practice. I have included tips for working through some blocks and difficulties which you may encounter, and my first "ninety in ninety" days of meditation messages, as an example of the results you can get through practicing prayer and meditation in your daily life.

Several quotes from Twelve Step literature are included, to point out some of the frequent passages that emphasize the importance of prayer and meditation in a recovery program.

I conclude with some of the amazing beneficial changes I have experienced as a result of the consistent practice of prayer and meditation, as well as statements from important people in my life regarding the changes they have observed in me.

Using prayer and meditation to improve my connection with God has transformed my life. As I continue to improve my connection with God, I find myself being of more value to my fellows. As a result, all of my relationships have improved, including the one I have with myself. My life is much more enjoyable and satisfying today.

I hope that this example of my experience with prayer and meditation aids you in realizing the promises in the book *Alcoholics Anonymous*. "We begin to feel the nearness of our Creator. We may have had certain spiritual beliefs, but now we begin to have a spiritual experience … We feel we are on the Broad Highway, walking hand in hand with the Spirit of the Universe."[4]

Practicing Step 11 will help you develop your relationship with God and live more closely aligned with God's will.

Whether you're new to mediation or you've been meditating for some time, I hope you find tools and suggestions in this book that will help you embrace the many blessings that await you on this amazing journey!

ACKNOWLEDGMENTS

Thanks for making this book possible go to God. I am grateful God gave me the words in this book and the ability to write it.

Tom R., my mentor and my teacher. Thank you for sharing your knowledge and for giving me the tools that helped me create a strong connection with God. Practicing what you taught me has improved both the quality of my life and the person I am becoming. Your teachings have had a remarkable, positive, life-changing impact on me.

Jessi R., my first prayer and meditation partner. Thank you for helping me make prayer and meditation a part of my daily life. I am honored that you shared with me your intimate conversations with God, during my first "ninety in ninety" days prayer and meditation commitment.

My husband, Craig, and my son, Steven. Thank you for all of your support and patience during the times I slipped and went "off my meds" (meditations). Thank you for holding a mirror up to me, so I could see both the positive and negative results of my choices regarding making my prayer and meditation time a priority in our lives. This book would not have been possible without the faith you had in me, your understanding, and your encouragement.

Dana K., Deborah C., and several other friends. Thank you for reading portions of my manuscript and giving me valuable feedback. Thank you for the time and effort you put into editing my words and helping me create a more polished final product.

INTRODUCTION

It is emphasized repeatedly in the book *Alcoholics Anonymous* that maintaining our spiritual condition is a requirement for staying sober.

In discussing Step 10, *Alcoholics Anonymous* states that after working Steps 1 through 9, we will no longer have a problem with alcohol. However, it then gives us this warning:

> It is easy to let up on the spiritual program of *action* ... We are headed for trouble if we do, for alcohol is a subtle foe. We are not cured of alcoholism. What we really have is a daily reprieve contingent on the maintenance of our spiritual condition.[5]

Step 11 in *Alcoholics Anonymous* suggests daily prayer and meditation. Emmet Fox, who is described as being one of the most influential spiritual leaders of this century, tells us how to enlarge our spiritual life. "There is only one way to make spiritual progress, and that is to practice the Presence of God."[6] In meditation, you will improve your ability to seek, to make contact with, and to fully experience the presence of God.

After practicing Step 11 daily for several years, I now understand why the early members of AA said that the awareness of God's presence was the most important aspect of their lives. I have learned to sit quietly and enjoy just being in God's presence, without having to do or say anything. My ability to be comfortable while quietly enjoying a connection with God continues to improve, through my daily prayer and meditation practice.

PART 1

MY LIFE PRIOR TO MEDITATION

CHAPTER 1

MY BRAIN INJURY

Following the program outlined in the book *Alcoholics Anonymous* has enabled me to experience a remarkable recovery, mentally and spiritually. This book will describe my progression from an almost hopeless condition to my current position as a business owner, pilot, and author. I offer my story as an example of what someone can accomplish through using the tools of a Twelve Step program, including practicing Step 11 consistently.

On July 5, 1984, my fiancé was driving us into town when we were in an automobile accident with a drunk driver in a pickup truck. The truck hit us head-on and then drove over the top of our car, compressing the roof. From measuring the distance between our wrecked car and where the truck came to rest, the police determined that the combined impact was approximately 110 mph.

I was taken to the nearest hospital and diagnosed with having sustained a severe concussion and a brain contusion (bruising of the brain), along with other physical damage. I was admitted with a 10 percent chance of living.

I was in a coma for several days. When the doctors could communicate with me, they told me my brain injury was so severe that I would never again be employable and that I would need social security disability payments to help support me for the remainder of my life.

They also told me that I had multiple breaks of my left arm, and my pelvis had separated in the accident. I had been unable to move my left hand or any part of my right leg or right foot since arriving at the hospital. After explaining to me how bad my condition was, the doctor ended by telling me, "Oh, and your fiancé died in the accident."

Because my brain had been so badly damaged, I had no memories of my life prior to the accident. (This is referred to as "long-term memory"). The people who visited me in the hospital included my employer and some of my dance students. I learned from them that I had worked as a custom jeweler in a jewelry store at a local mall. I had also taught weekly dance classes and performed frequently in local events with a troupe of my advanced students. It got very depressing to hear about the beautiful life I was no longer going to be able to live.

Weeks later, I was released from the hospital with home nursing service and only a 50 percent chance of living. They sent me home because the medical staff had done everything they could for me, there was no further treatment available for me, and they needed the bed space.

My parents were told that the staff had never, in the history of the hospital, seen anyone survive after being hurt as badly as I had been. They weren't sure why I didn't die or how long I would be able to stay alive, and they had no recovery program available to help me regain the mental abilities I would need to take care of myself.

I was told I would need nursing care at least for the foreseeable future and possibly for the rest of my life, but with time and recovery, it was possible that I might become "capable of self-care."

The doctors arranged for me to have physical therapy, in hopes that I could regain at least partial use of my disabled body parts. I complained that I would need both of my hands to make jewelry and both of my legs to dance, so I could start earning a living again. The doctors explained that they were quite certain I would never be able to remember how to make jewelry or dance again, so it didn't really matter if I could use my left hand or right leg. They encouraged me to think of sitting on the couch and watching TV while collecting social security disability payments as a "paid vacation."

For several weeks, my nurse chauffeured me to an average of seven doctor appointments a week. She helped me perform my physical therapy exercises and tried to teach me how to take care of myself and my apartment.

Unfortunately, my ability to retain memories (short-term memory) had also been severely damaged. I continually forgot what the nurse taught me. On a daily basis, my nurse had to teach me how to brush my teeth, etc., as if it was a brand-new lesson each time.

I experienced constant frustration with trying to do things for myself and wanting to return to my previous lifestyle. Because I kept insisting I could learn to live independently, I was sent to a psychiatrist. It states in my medical file, "The patient is deluding herself ... which is detrimental to her eventual, possible recovery."

My pain medications were not effectively blocking the pain I was experiencing as a result of my injuries. I was worn out from dealing with physical pain, the heartache of losing my fiancé, and trying to cope with the results of my brain injury. I began to have an overwhelming feeling of hopelessness, and I found myself wanting to drink.

I had never been told that both of my parents were adult children of alcoholics who had decided that they did not want to become like their parents and never drank alcohol problematically. They were ashamed there was alcoholism in their families, so they had hidden that fact from me while I was growing up.

I realize now that I was craving alcohol after the accident, but at that time, I had no knowledge about the disease of alcoholism or its symptoms (and I had no memories regarding my own drinking pattern prior to the accident). I found ways to sneak away from my nurse and get alcohol from different neighbors in my apartment complex.

When someone's brain gets bruised from impacting the inside of the skull, it swells. The swollen brain pressing against the inside of the skull causes further mental problems, adding to the original damage. It takes between two and three years for the swelling to completely subside. Medical literature states that your brain is "incapable of tolerating alcohol" while you are recovering from a brain injury.

Things got very ugly very fast!

After a short time, the nursing service refused to continue caring for me. I was moved into my parents' home in Washington because I was incapable of living alone, and there wasn't any service or organization that was willing to assume responsibility for my care.

During the first few months after my accident, my parents took me to eight different doctors, hoping to find a possible path of recovery. However, all of their findings confirmed the original gloomy prognosis.

As a last resort, my parents contacted the State of Washington Head Injury Foundation to have me examined by their lead neuropsychologist. After eight hours of testing, his conclusion confirmed that I would never be employable, that it was unlikely that I would ever be capable of self-care, and that I would need my disability payments to continue for the rest of my life.

My parents were given one piece of good news. They were told that as the swelling of my brain went down, it might become possible for some of my mental abilities and memories to return.

After several months, I did get to the point where periodically a memory of my dead fiancé would come back. I wasn't trying to remember the time I spent with David; these memories would just randomly pop into my mind. The sadness I experienced while dealing with these "new" memories also made me want to drink alcohol to numb the emotional pain.

My parents knew I wasn't supposed to drink alcohol, but I kept saying, "If you hurt as badly as I do, you'd want a drink too!" I began sneaking away to get alcohol again. At one point, I drank myself back into a coma and was nonresponsive for three days.

Being able to live a life of value was looking like a hopeless dream. None of the doctors believed I would ever be anything other than a burden to my family and someone who needed to be taken care of for the remainder of her life. It was easy to consider giving up and losing my entire life in a bottle.

CHAPTER 2

MY MENTAL AND PHYSICAL RECOVERY

Luckily, I found my way into the rooms of Alcoholics Anonymous and was introduced to a Twelve Step program of recovery. God started doing for me what no human power could.

When my parents contacted the State of Washington Head Injury Foundation, we were given exercises I could do to help develop my memory. I started doing the memory exercises many times every day, along with my physical-therapy exercises. I just continued doing the next indicated step on a daily basis, walking in faith. Over time, I managed to recover almost completely from my brain injury.

The Head Injury Foundation suggests that where there is loss of memory related to skills required for source of income, the victim of a brain injury should be exposed to the equipment used in his or her job-related activities to help stimulate memory recall.

I read books on making jewelry and looked through many jewelry-tool catalogs, noting which tools were listed in the stone-setting section, etc. I bought jeweler's tools, and I spent a lot of time just holding them in my hands, trying to remember what I used to do with them. After some of my memories returned, we built a jeweler's workbench in the garage, where I spent time attempting to do simple jewelry projects. That helped trigger more memories.

After I regained my jewelry skills, I carved two custom waxes of the Greek letter psi, for psychologist. Then I used the lost wax casting method of jewelry manufacture to make two tie tacks for the head-injury expert who had examined me—who had concluded I would never again be employable.

I mailed the tie tacks to him, along with a note requesting that he consider holding out at least some hope for the patients he examines in the future. I explained that if I had believed his prognosis, it would have been impossible for me to create the jewelry he was being given.

That doctor was amazed at my accomplishment and wrote me back. We communicated for several months. He started referring to me as a "miracle patient" and telling my story to the families of patients who had a negative prognosis, to give them hope in what appears to be a hopeless situation.

That is a very generous answer to the prayer I cried out so often during my recovery—wanting my life to be of some value somewhere, somehow, to someone. I had only been hoping to possibly hold down some kind of part-time job, but now my story is being used to give hope to victims of head injuries and their families!

I used the same process of exposing myself to things I had previously done, to bring back memories of how to drive, to use a keyboard for typing, etc. Over time, I did regain the majority of my long-term memories, and I improved my ability to retain short-term memories.

As strange as this sounds, I am grateful for that accident. During my recovery, I learned some extremely valuable lessons, including that God answers prayers much more generously than we can imagine if we let Him. Today I'm working on not limiting what God wants to do with my life.

PART 2

PRACTICING PRAYER AND MEDITATION

CHAPTER 3

MY SPIRITUAL RECOVERY

By 2010, my life was pretty good. I was grateful for how much my mental abilities had improved, for my physical rehabilitation, and for my Twelve Step recovery. However, I struggled with ongoing random memory loss and problems with orientation. Living on life's terms was a constant source of frustration. I dealt with a lot of anger and resentment about having to handle the daily problems that occur as a result of mental limitations.

Another result of having incurred a brain injury is a limited ability to control or moderate emotions. Negative emotions would frequently overwhelm me. I couldn't subdue my emotions with logic, by telling myself that continuing with a train of thought was pointless, etc. I had no way to prevent the emotion I was experiencing from enlarging. When that happened, I couldn't focus on what I was doing, which would make more problems occur (not registering where I parked my car, not remembering to put my debit card back in my purse before I left a store, etc.).

I didn't have many friends, because I wasn't comfortable to be around. Many people have told me that I used to scare them. In fact, I earned the nickname "Crazy Cathy" due to my lack of emotional control and my frequent episodes of spontaneous, inappropriate behavior.

At fourteen years sober, I had worked all of the steps of my Twelve Step program with three different sponsors, including multiple fourth steps on my persistent "justifiable resentments," but emotional sobriety was evading me.

Then I attended my first prayer and meditation workshop, and I was given the tools I needed to create a strong connection with God. This spiritual experience has remarkably improved my level of acceptance, and my life. The negative effects of my brain injury have decreased significantly since I have been consistently practicing prayer and meditation. I believe a big part of that is because practicing Step 11 is helping me have more emotional balance.

Emotional balance is one of the results of meditation, as stated in our Twelve Step literature.

> And let's always remember that meditation is in reality intensely practical. One of its first fruits is emotional balance. With it we can broaden and deepen the channel between ourselves and God as we understand Him.[7]

Because I am experiencing more emotional balance now, I rarely allow myself to become overwhelmed by frustration due to my memory problems. When I'm not distracted by strong emotions, I can actually focus on what it is that I am doing. Being more fully present makes me more effective—and because my brain registers what I am doing more fully, I remember more.

My ability to retain memories continues to improve, as well as my ability to navigate. I now register where I park my car and how to get to and from different places much more often than what was previously possible. The many improvements I am experiencing are making my life much easier and much better.

Because I am more comfortable with myself, and I am enjoying my life so much more, people enjoy having me in their lives more. Today, I try to always be a source of positive energy and good emotions. I am much more successful at achieving that goal, because I am consistently practicing prayer and meditation.

When I start my day feeling connected to God and my fellows, I am much less likely to let selfishness and self-centeredness create problems in my life and drama in my relationships. I've changed from being very focused on myself, my life, and my problems to really caring about and feeling connected to others.

I am more able to help others when I'm following God's directions. When I see myself being of value to others, it improves my self-esteem. All of that is God's will for me.

Practicing Step 11 has also changed how successful I am at my job, especially when I have to interact with clients and personnel. I believe that I make better choices today regarding how I choose to communicate, how I choose to show up in each situation, and how I approach problems. As a result, my work relationships have all benefitted from my prayer and meditation practice.

Because my brain was so badly damaged during the accident, all of the doctors involved with my case agreed that there was no hope for me to recover. Today, I am using the tools of my Twelve Step program, including practicing Step 11 consistently, to create a life that is full, rich, rewarding, and enjoyable. I live a blessed life today, but I do the daily work to help create it and to maintain it.

Finding time to pray and meditate each day, no matter what, is turning my life into a beautiful adventure filled with love, hope, and purpose. I have regained everything that I lost, and I have added much more to my life, through prayer and meditation. I have recovered physically, mentally, and spiritually from seemingly hopeless conditions. I am living the promises!

I am not only employed now, which the doctors thought was impossible, but my husband and I run a corporation that has grown an average of 41 percent per year over the past ten years. We provide work to more than twenty subcontractors. I am in charge of hiring, managing, and running the quality control program and payroll for all of our subcontractors, as well as invoicing all of our clients.

I teach weekly dance classes again and occasionally perform. Additionally, I have participated in several 5K runs, raising money for different charities. That is a real success story for me, since it took several months of appointments with doctors and physical therapy to regain use of my right leg.

The doctors didn't believe that I would ever become capable of self-care, let alone be able to raise a child. I am proud to say that my son has grown into a wonderful young man who has learned both the benefits of a Twelve Step program and of a consistent prayer and meditation practice by observing me. My son just graduated with a degree in psychology. He wants to become a counselor so he can help people. Because of the work I am doing to improve my life, my son has called me his "hero and role model."

Despite the doctors' prognosis, I managed to remember and regain the skills I need to make jewelry. My son recently asked me to create a custom-made engagement ring and wedding band set for his fiancée. It means a great deal to me that my son wants his wife to wear jewelry that I created. My son and I enjoy a respectful and enjoyable relationship today. I don't think "The Family After" chapter in the book *Alcoholics Anonymous* has a story better than mine!

I am happy to say that I live a very active life today, which includes motorcycling and paragliding. I don't believe that I could ride my motorcycle and fly my paraglider safely if I did not have the ability to quiet my mind and focus on my current moment, which is something that I learned, and am continuing to improve, during my meditation practice.

My recovery from this accident and my adventure with prayer and meditation have taught me that if you try daily to turn your will and your life over to the care of God, there are *no limitations* to what you can accomplish. With God directing my life today, the sky isn't even the limit for me.

Paraglider flying over mountains

When I was trying to recover from the mental and physical effects of the accident, I used to pray to God to help me have a life worth living. God has answered my prayer far more generously than I could have imagined! I absolutely believe that God will do the same for each and every one of us … *if He is sought.*

CHAPTER 4

FOCUSED MEDITATION

During my first weekend prayer and meditation retreat, the leader of the event, Tom R., guided us through several meditations. We were given the information he has outlined in his book *Prayer and Meditation: A Practical Guide to the Life Promised in Step 11*. (This is available through www. PracticallySpiritualBooks.com.)

During the weekend exercises, I found a way to connect to my Higher Power and to feel God's presence, I learned to ask for and *receive* messages when I meditated, and I also learned to relax and really enjoy the experience.

In his introduction, Tom R. stated that many alcoholics have problems with styles of meditation that tell you to start with a "blank" mind. He said, "Alcoholics don't do blank minds." That got my attention! I thought, *He understands the problem, but does he have a solution?*

I discovered he has an approach to meditation that works for me, and for many others who have tried it.

I learned during the first meditations of the retreat that although I can't empty my mind of thoughts, I *can* focus on just one word or one thought at a time. This limits how much attention is available for other distracting thoughts.

To do this type of focused meditation, pick a meaningful phrase, such as "God loves me," and focus on the meaning of each word while repeating it over and over. Repeating a phrase while focusing on the meaning of each word helps you fully "digest" the words. While you're engaged in this process of repetition and reflection, the concept behind the words makes the journey from your mind into your heart and then sinks into the core of your being. This is like repeating the multiplication tables until you know them by heart.

CHAPTER 5

EXAMPLE MEDITATION

Before you spend any (more) time in prayer and meditation, it would be beneficial to take time to define *your* concept of God, so you have a clear idea of what it is that you are trying to bring more fully into your life through practicing Step 11.

You might want to get a piece of paper for this exercise and write down things that the word *God* means to you, such as Creator of the Universe, Father of Light, and source of all goodness and love. You could also write down a list of adjectives, such as kind, loving, and forgiving.

Remember that this list is specifically tailored to outline *your* beliefs about God. Don't just write down things that you have read or heard about "God." Search your heart, and describe the God of your beliefs.

Many people find that it also helps to write down a list of what their God is not (e.g., punishing, demanding, cruel, and vengeful).

Once you have created a definition of what your God is, and what your God is not, then you will have a clear concept of what it is you are trying to connect with during your prayer and meditation time.

"God Loves Me" Meditation

I could never sit still and meditate for even five minutes until I worked with this technique. My mind quiets down when I practice this style of meditation, because it requires a significant amount of thought process to focus my mind on the meaning and significance of each word. Eventually, I stop being distracted by the multiple thoughts that usually flitter around inside my brain, demanding attention. It works! It really does.

In this form of focused meditation, you start by emphasizing the first word while repeating the phrase several times: *God* loves me. God—Creator, Heavenly Father, Spirit of the Universe, source of all goodness and love, etc.—loves me. *God* loves me. Repeat the phrase over and over again for a minute or two, focusing on and absorbing the meaning of the word *God*.

Then move to the next word of the phrase and emphasize it, while repeating the phrase several more times: God (remembering what that word means and how it feels to focus on that word) *loves*—cherishes, adores, treasures, etc.—me. God *loves* me. Repeat the phrase while focusing on the feeling and the meaning of the word *loves* for a minute or two.

Next, focus on and emphasize the third word of the phrase: *me*. Think about who you are and how you became the person you are today. God loves you despite all of the dark secrets that you feel you have to hide from others, in order to be a "lovable" person. God knows everything about you and about what made you who you are today. He knows your faults and weakness as well as your strengths and beauty—and God loves you, just as you are. Repeat the phrase for a minute or two longer, while focusing on the word *me*. God loves *me*.

Finally, repeat the entire phrase while reflecting on the meaning of each and every word as you repeat it, for another minute or two. *God loves me. God* (remembering the meaning of the word) *loves* (remembering the feeling of the word) *me*, focusing on the entire package of who you are, which isn't just acceptable to God; it's lovable. *God loves me!* You *are* good enough for God to love, unconditionally.

Before you know it, you will have meditated for five minutes or more. Repeating "God loves me" (or another significant phrase), while focusing on the meaning of the words, helps quiet and focus your mind while giving you time to digest the meaning of the phrase at a deep level.

Extended Meditation

When you're ready to expand your meditation time, start with a focused meditation, to clear and center your mind. Then ask God what He wants to communicate to you and sit quietly for a few minutes, writing down whatever comes into your mind. This is asking God to speak to you, then listening for a while and writing down what you think you hear.

Step 11 in the book *Alcoholics Anonymous* instructs us to "ask God" several times. It doesn't make sense that we are told to "ask God" over and over again, if it weren't possible for us to receive a response. Meditation is a time when we stop to listen for God's response to our prayers.

In one of my first meditations, after I asked God what He wanted to say to me, I got a visual image of myself rowing a small boat with a flat front. I was really struggling to move forward, because the front of the boat was meeting so much resistance from the water. Then a pointed prow with the word "God" written on it floated down from the sky and locked itself onto the front of my boat. After that, I smoothly cut through the water without any struggle, and without causing any turbulence in the water around me.

During that meditation, I got the message that if I put God in front of my plans for the day, I won't need to put so much energy into whatever I do. Also, if I keep remembering to put God first, I won't create so much commotion and turbulence in the lives of the people around me.

That was a clear picture to me of how to use prayer and meditation first thing in the morning, to set the tone for my day, as well as throughout the day. Any time I find myself struggling, I can pause and ask, "Have I tried to step around God and take over running the day by myself?" When I remember to put God first, my day's journey is much smoother and less tiring.

That early meditation experience was an awakening for me. I had found a way to create a connection with God that produced a two-way communication. The pointed "God prow" on my boat idea was far too good to have come from my brain—that was a communication from my Higher Power. How exciting! That experience inspired me to learn more about the practice of meditation.

CHAPTER 6

SETTING THE STAGE FOR GOD'S APPEARANCE

Step 11 in the book *Alcoholics Anonymous* suggests that as soon as we awaken, we stop and think about whatever we have planned for the day. We are then instructed to ask God to guide our thinking, so our actions throughout the day can be more aligned with God's will.[8]

Many people find that it's best to meditate first thing in the morning, before all the busyness of the day starts.

Although *Alcoholics Anonymous* encourages us to meditate first thing in the morning, if your schedule makes that so stressful that you don't enjoy the process, you probably won't continue. If that is your situation, I suggest you keep your Step 11 work in the morning brief, and find a more comfortable time that fits your lifestyle to do longer meditations.

Setting aside a specific time of day for your meditations puts it on your schedule of things to do and makes it a part of your daily routine. If you arrange your schedule to meditate at the same time every day, it won't slip your mind. It's easy to forget, if your mediation time doesn't follow a consistent pattern.

Possibly you could set a few minutes aside when you return home from work, or find another time that could easily become habitual. I know a woman who just does a quick prayer in the morning, as her Step 11 practice. After she drives home from work, she does a full meditation in her car. She does this to center herself and align herself with God's will, before she starts her evening time with her family.

One day she was feeling selfish for setting that time aside for herself, and she apologized to her family. However, everyone in the family was so pleased with her being a calmer and happier person, they all encouraged her to continue with her evening meditation practice.

I like to meditate first thing in the morning, because that helps me put God's will for my day in front of my planned agenda. That's when I set myself (my ego, my feelings, and my ideas) aside and invite God in. If I check in with God first thing in the morning, it helps me stay on the path that God wants me to travel throughout my day.

If finding time in the morning is too difficult for you, don't give up. Keep changing your approach, juggling your timing and your conditions, and start with trying to find just five minutes for your meditation practice. New habits are hard to form, but starting with just five minutes a day is something most people can manage.

You should try to find someplace to meditate where you can relax and where you won't be interrupted. Some people like to set aside a special area where they do all of their meditations, so that particular setting becomes their place to connect with God. You might want to create a space in your home with a spiritual feeling to it, using candles or whatever else helps you experience an open and receptive frame of mind. Alternatively, you could imagine that you are in a spiritual setting.

God's Room Meditation: Imagine a room where God meets with you, and only with you. God meets with other people in their God rooms—your God room is a place where only you and God meet to spend time with each other. You can make it whatever you want, and you can change the setting or furnishings any time you choose.

Your God room can be a cozy library with overstuffed furniture and a warm fireplace, it can look like the room where your grandmother used to tell you stories when you were a kid, or it can be a grass hut on a tropical beach where you lie in a hammock and listen to the waves crash against the shore. Create something that works for you.

You can use your imagination to go to your God room whenever you meditate, whenever you feel stressed, or whenever you just want to soak in God's presence—any time throughout your day.

Prepare the supplies you need: pen and paper (or a meditation journal) and perhaps something to drink. It's easier to focus on being connected with God if you're not tense, so you should also gather whatever will help you feel more comfortable when you meditate, such as a blanket and pillow. You might want to play inspirational music while you meditate, etc. As you settle into your meditation area, get into a comfortable position and relax.

If you think you might be distracted by having to watch the time, due to your schedule, set a timer. I suggest that you start with only five minutes, because you want to make meditation easy to manage at first. I wound up enjoying the process so much that I kept adding more and more time, but I think you should add more time gradually so it doesn't become an inconvenient addition to your daily requirements and crowd your schedule too much. If it doesn't feel good, you probably won't continue with your meditation practice. Keep the time requirement within your comfort zone.

If you're someone who habitually has a lot of interrupting thoughts about the many important things you should be doing instead of spending time meditating, you might want to have a separate piece of paper close by. When those "things to do" items pop into your mind while you're trying to meditate, just jot them down and return to your meditation practice.

You will be better able to receive God's communications if you are not thinking about the things you have to do later on in the day. It will be easier to set those things aside if you write them down, so you won't be distracted by worrying about whether you will forget to do something that you feel is important.

Finally, let go of trying to control your meditation experience and let God be in control. Let go; let God.

CHAPTER 7

KEEP IT SIMPLE

Meditation isn't really all that mysterious, mystical, or complicated. A simple outline to use for your meditation practice is this: *pray, read, meditate, write,* and *share.*

Pray. Praying is when we talk to God. Meditating is when we listen for His response. It's good to start your meditation session by saying a prayer that is meaningful to you, to open the channel of communication between you and God, and to establish your intention. Be sure to reflect on the meaning of each word, so that you are *praying* the prayer, rather than just *saying* the words.

You can choose a prayer that is associated with your specific religion, such as the Lord's Prayer. Alternatively, you could begin by praying the Third Step Prayer and/or the Seventh Step Prayer, from the book *Alcoholics Anonymous.*

Third Step Prayer

God, I offer myself to Thee—to build with me
and to do with me as Thou wilt. Relieve me of
the bondage of self, that I may better do Thy
will. Take away my difficulties, that victory
over them may bear witness to those I would
help of Thy Power, Thy Love, and Thy Way of
life. May I do Thy will always![8]

Seventh Step Prayer

My Creator, I am now willing that you should
have all of me, good and bad. I pray that you now
remove from me every single defect of character
which stands in the way of my usefulness to you
and my fellows. Grant me strength, as I go out
from here, to do your bidding. Amen.[9]

Follow your prayer or prayers with asking God to speak to
you. You can ask for God's answer to a specific problem that
you're having or for His reply to a specific question. Asking
God, "What do You want to say to me today?" or "How can
I be an instrument of Your will today?" is a good way to start
a conversation with God.

While you sit quietly waiting for God's answer, focus on
God. Don't focus on yourself and what is going on in your
mind. Don't hope for a specific communication; just focus on
God. Listen for God's message, with pen in hand.

Read. If I'm not hearing anything from God, I might use
something that I've read to start a conversation. This is
equivalent to breaking the ice at a party where you don't really

know anyone, by asking something like "How about that game Sunday?" You might get into a fascinating conversation, where you learn some very interesting facts, but you have to get the conversational ball rolling first.

You can use literature associated with your religious affiliation to inspire a meditation or read Step 11 in the book *Alcoholics Anonymous.* Those pages include a detailed description of what we should do before we go to sleep and when we wake up, to improve our connection with God and open a door for communication.

There are many spiritual ideas presented in the book *Alcoholics Anonymous* that can be used as the basis for meditations. For example, the discussion of Step 10 includes this statement: "We have entered the world of the Spirit. Our next function is to grow in understanding and effectiveness. This is not an overnight matter."[10] It then suggests that we continue to take a daily inventory, continually watching for defects of character. It states that when we observe a negative trait, we should immediately ask God to remove it. You could start a meditation with a prayer for God to help you deal with one of those issues.

Reading one of the many books that are available in the "spiritual literature" category, such as one of the books that has a different spiritual thought for each day of the year, can also give you a focus for a meditation.

When selecting a book to inspire your meditations, check to be sure that the content is in line with the principles of your Twelve Step program.

Meditate. Repeat the phrase you selected over and over, fully digesting the meaning of the words, or focus on an idea that you found in your reading material. Do this to slow down and focus your mind on just one thought, instead of being distracted by the multiple random thoughts that pop into a busy, unfocused brain.

Write. After meditating on your chosen idea for a while, sit quietly for five to ten minutes. During this time, reflect on your connection with God and what God might want to communicate to you at this time. After a few minutes of quiet time, start writing whatever comes to mind.

If you don't seem to get any messages at the beginning of your mediation, you might ask God what He wants you to get out of today's reading material or prayer.

Write down whatever comes into your mind, without editing. Don't judge thoughts as not being good enough to write down; just go with the flow. This is a stream-of-consciousness exercise. Sometimes my pen will write something that I hadn't realized I needed to address. God can give you interesting things to look at, if you open the door and don't block any of the ideas that come. Being judgmental about whether you are meditating properly can limit what you get out of your conversation with God.

For me, the "magic" to hearing from God is in the writing. Over the years, I've found that the days when I don't make time to write, I don't feel as full a connection to my Higher Power and I don't get really good messages. Asking for a communication from God isn't like placing an order at a fast-food window; messages from God aren't guaranteed to come "in five minutes, or it's free." You need to spend time developing your ability to listen.

Share. It is a good idea for everyone who is starting to make prayer and meditation a daily routine to work with a partner. Because it takes a while to develop a habit, it is recommended that you and a buddy agree to do "ninety in ninety"—ninety meditations in ninety days. For ninety days, no matter what is going on in your life, you both make time to pray and meditate. Every day, you each share what you got out of your prayer and meditation session with your partner.

In my meditation sessions, after I finish my spiritual writing, I look over what I have written and decide what it means to me. When such things as "call your sponsor" are written down, I don't share those action items with anyone. However, sometimes I get impactful messages that inspire others when I share them. At other times, I just get feelings of gratitude and of connection to all others and to all of creation. Whatever I decide is worth sharing gets emailed or texted to my prayer and meditation buddies.

Frequently, when I restate what I got during meditation, it gives me a better perspective of the message. Reviewing it, and writing it so that it makes sense for another person, puts the message I received more into focus for me.

Pray to connect.
Read to inspire.
Meditate to focus.
Write to listen and receive.
Share to clarify and help others.

CHAPTER 8

PRAYER AND MEDITATION IN A TWELVE STEP PROGRAM

In Twelve Step programs, we use prayer and meditation to establish a *two-way* communication with God. This is from the book *Alcoholics Anonymous*: **"Step 11**—Sought through prayer and meditation to improve our conscious contact with God *as we understood Him*, praying only for knowledge of His will for us and the power to carry that out."[11] (Note: This prayer has two parts. The first part is for *knowledge* of God's will, and the second part is for the *power* to carry that out.)

The instructions in Step 11 are to spend time in meditation every morning, trying to align yourself with God's will. You can start your meditation by praying for the knowledge of God's will for you. Ask God what your purpose is and how you can fulfill that purpose, just for today.

Dramatic differences can be observed when individuals who are working a recovery program make a connection with their Higher Power. The book *Alcoholics Anonymous* states it this way: "They found that a new power, peace, happiness and sense of direction flowed into them."[12] God wants us all to feel that way.

There are examples of God's will for us throughout AA literature. Promises of the fruits of working a program of recovery occur on almost every page in *Alcoholics Anonymous*. Every "promise" is an example of God's will for us.

The Serenity Prayer asks God to grant you three things: "God grant me the *serenity* to accept the things I cannot change, the *courage* to change the things I can, and the *wisdom* to know the difference." Those are all God's will for you.

God's Will Meditation

The God's Will Meditation requires writing. Get some paper, or start a meditation journal, and write, "God's will for me is ..." at the top of a page. After centering your mind, sit quietly for a few minutes and jot down everything you believe that God wants for you (happiness, joy, freedom from bondage, a new power, a sense of direction, serenity, courage, wisdom, etc.)

After you have a list of what you believe is God's will for you, you can do a meditation on each item listed, asking, "God, grant me _____."

As previously outlined in chapter 5, repeat the phrase several times while focusing on the meaning of each word in turn, until you have emphasized each word of the phrase several times.

- "*GOD,* grant me serenity."
- "God, *GRANT* me serenity."
- "God, grant *ME* serenity."
- "God, grant me *SERENITY.*"

CATHY C.

Shift your focus from one word to the next, meditating on the meaning of each word until you have absorbed the meaning of each word of the phrase.

Follow that process with slowly repeating the entire phrase, focusing on the meaning of each and every word as you say it. *"God, grant me serenity."* This meditation should take approximately five minutes.

After focusing on your chosen phrase for a few minutes (to quiet your mind), you can expand the meditation by sitting quietly for five to ten minutes—listening for God's voice and writing what you hear. God may have a message for you regarding serenity (or whatever the topic of your meditation was), or you may hear God speak to you about something entirely different.

Remain open to God, and write down the thoughts and feelings that come to you during your listening time. Practicing listening will improve your two-way communications with God.

These are examples of what I hear in my meditations, when I ask to be shown God's will for me:

- Embrace the joy and the beauty of this day. Learn to gracefully receive the blessings that God places in your life today.
- Let go of all thoughts that include self-pity. Choose to be happy.
- Think of others. Stay out of self-centeredness. Ask, "What can I do for another?" throughout the day.

As another round of meditations, you can go back over your same list of God's will for you, stating, "God *is my* _____." (For example, from the Serenity Prayer: "God *is my* serenity,"

36

"God *is my* courage," and "God *is my* wisdom.") As previously outlined, repeat the new phrase several times while focusing on the meaning of each word in turn, until you have emphasized each and every word of the new phrase several times.

- *"GOD* (Heavenly Father, Creator, etc.) is my serenity."
- "God *IS* (He exists; God is real for me) my serenity."
- "God is *MY* (it belongs to me; it is part of who I am) serenity."
- "God is my *SERENITY* (peace, untroubled state of calm, etc.)."
- *"God is my serenity,"* focusing on the meaning of each and every word, as you repeat the phrase.

You can use each word or idea on your list of "God's will" as the basis for two separate meditations: "God grant me _____," then "God is my _____."

Repeating these phrases over and over again will positively reinforce your intention to live God's will and to trust God to provide for you. During this process, the ideas in your brain become concepts that you know by heart, through repetition. You are learning God's will for you and that God will provide for you, deep in the core of your being, while you are improving your connection with God.

Before you end your God's Will Meditation, ask Him for the strength to do His will. If you make it a habit to pause throughout your day and pray for the knowledge of God's will for you *and* the power to carry it out, you will more fully experience the promises of your Twelve Step program.

CHAPTER 9

MEDITATE THROUGHOUT THE DAY

Develop the practice of pausing frequently during the day, to check that your thoughts and actions are in line with God's plans. If you correct a wrong course of action in a timely manner, and keep trying to live according to what you learn is God's will for you, your life will improve.

Many people I know take several five-minute breaks throughout their day, for short meditations. Others have their computer or cell-phone screens set to periodically display "God's will, not mine", as a constant reminder. Find a system that works for you.

If you analyze the instructions included in Step 11, in the chapter titled "Into Action" in *Alcoholics Anonymous*, you will find specific directions to follow throughout your entire day, such as the following:

- Consider your upcoming plans.
- Pause when you are upset or confused.
- Ask God to guide you.
- Ask for inspiration.

- Relax.
- Ask God to show you what the next step is to be.
- Rely on God to give you direction.
- Ask for the power to take the next indicated step.[13]

Learning to follow these suggestions will reduce the amount of unhappiness, frustration, relationship problems, drama, and chaos in your life.

It takes time to develop the habit of continuing to seek God's will throughout the day. Practice making yourself pause to ask for God's direction before you respond to a situation. Ask God, "What is it you would like me to say right now?" or "What should I do right now?" Then wait and listen for God's answer. (Sometimes the answer is "Nothing." Nothing can be the right answer.)

Prayer and meditation is an exercise program to improve the condition of your soul. (Daily spiritual exercise is recommended.) When your soul is in good shape, you are more prepared to live a life that feels good and has value.

Through experience, I have come to believe that if you try to live your life in accordance with God's will—your life will grow to be bigger, fuller, more enjoyable, and more meaningful. You will be a better tool in God's hands, when you try to live according to how He designed you to work. The result is that you will become more useful and valuable to others. That leads to greater self-esteem.

When I meditate and open myself to hear God, and follow the instructions I receive, I feel that I am living a life with a good purpose—a life that has value. That is an amazing place to be, especially given my condition after my debilitating accident!

CHAPTER 10

THE NEED FOR MEDITATION

We have to work the program, to get the promises of the program. Several passages from our AA literature discuss the beneficial results of prayer and meditation. Consistently practicing prayer and meditation, as outlined in Step 11, gives you the ability to experience the promises outlined in the book *Alcoholics Anonymous*.

Many recovering alcoholics have learned the hard way that most of our problems occur because we operate on self-will rather than God's will. We also find that we need God's help to remove our defects of character—that struggle as we might, we can't seem to rid ourselves of defects, such as self-centeredness and selfish motives, without God's help.

Many people who practice Step 11 daily have been pleased to discover that as they continue using prayer and meditation to improve their spiritual life, their troubles begin to diminish. Setting self aside, asking for God's guidance and then trying to follow God's will throughout the day cannot help but create a better life.

Practicing prayer and meditation consistently will also help you develop a sense of serenity, which is defined as "a peaceful state of untroubled calm."

After you have established a routine of prayer and meditation, you will definitely notice a negative effect if you miss a few days, as described in this passage from *Alcoholics Anonymous*:

> Those of us who have come to make regular use of prayer would no more do without it that we would refuse air, food, or sunshine ... When we refuse air, light, or food, the body suffers. And when we turn away from meditation and prayer, we likewise deprive our minds, our emotions, and our intuitions of vitally needed support.[14]

The more I get to know God, the more I learn about myself, and the more comfortable with myself I become. The more time I spend improving my relationship with God, the happier I become with myself. That somehow manages to extend into my relationships with other people. My entire life keeps improving as I continue with my Step 11 practice. I believe the same will be true for everyone who develops a consistent practice of prayer and meditation.

In the chapter "Freedom from Bondage," *Alcoholics Anonymous* states that the "basic problem was a spiritual hunger."[15] Think of your time spent in prayer and meditation as a time spent feeding your soul.

In the book *Twelve Steps and Twelve Traditions*, it states in the chapter on Step 11,

> We will want the good that is in us all, even in the worst of us, to flower and grow ... Most of all we shall want sunlight; nothing much can

grow in the dark. Meditation is our step out into the sun.[16]

Step, run, or dance into the sunlight of the Spirit each morning as you start your day, and watch how beautiful your life can become.

CHAPTER 11

IDEAS FOR MEDITATION

Prayers: You can use a prayer, or focus on just one line of a familiar prayer, as the basis for a meditation. For example, you could use the line from the Lord's Prayer "Thy will be done on earth as it is in Heaven" as the basis for your meditation one day.

The ideas presented in the Third Step Prayer and the Seventh Step Prayer, from the book *Alcoholics Anonymous*, make for good meditations. (These prayers are printed in chapter 7, which is titled "Keep It Simple.")

Any of the lines from the Prayer of St. Francis can be used for the basis of a meditation, such as "God, make me a channel of Thy peace." There are many versions of this prayer. The version I like follows.

Prayer of St. Francis

Lord, make me a channel of your peace;
that where there is hatred, I may bring love;
that where there is wrong, I may bring the spirit
of forgiveness;
that where there is discord, I may bring
harmony;
that where there is error, I may bring truth;
that where there is doubt, may I bring faith;
that where there is despair, I may bring hope;
that where there are shadows, I may bring light;
that where there is sadness, I may bring joy.

Lord, grant that I may seek to comfort rather
than be comforted;
to understand, rather than to be understood;
to love, rather than to be loved.
For it is by self-forgetting that one finds.
It is by forgiving that one is forgiven.
It is by dying that one awakens to eternal life.
Amen.

You can also meditate on any of the ideas contained in one
of the many other, less formal, prayers that can be found in the
book *Alcoholics Anonymous*. Every time it states, "Ask God," that
is a prayer. Read through *Alcoholics Anonymous*, and find your
favorite prayers.

Visualizations: If you combine using visualization along with
a meditation, it can make your meditation more meaningful
and effective.

You may want to visualize a "God box," a box in which you put all of your problems, so that God can take care of them while they are out of your sight and mind. As you meditate, if troublesome issues arise, imagine placing them in your God box and move on. (You may want to write these things down on pieces of paper and create an actual God box to use along with this process.)

Most of us experience problems with our minds wandering during meditation. Many styles of meditation suggest that when that happens, focusing on your breath for a while will help center your mind on just one thing. Several of my favorite meditations focus on receiving something good every time I inhale and releasing something negative every time I exhale. I use this process to connect my breath to my meditation, which helps keep my mind focused.

★ **Healing prayers**: Ask God, "Please heal me—even in those places where I don't even know that I'm wounded." When you do this meditation, imagine the healing power of God entering and filling your heart every time you inhale. Then, every beat of your heart pushes more of God's healing power throughout your bloodstream, replenishing and empowering every part of your body and your being. You may want to imagine this as a golden light coursing through your blood vessels.

When you exhale, focus on releasing tension and pain. You are not alone. God is with you, comforting you. Repeat this several times. After doing this meditation, know that you have filled yourself with reserves of God's strength, which you can draw on throughout your day.

I learned a "healing" version of the St. Francis Prayer at an AA Women's International Conference, and I enjoy using it as the source for meditations.

Healing Prayer

Lord,
Make me an instrument of your healing.
When I am weak and in pain, help me to rest.
When I am anxious, help me to wait.
When I am fearful, help me to trust.
When I am lonely, help me to love.
When I place you apart from me, help me to know that You are near.

Healing God,
Grant me not so much to demand everything from myself, as to let others help me,
nor to expect others to cure me, as to do my own part toward getting better.
Grant me not so much to seek escape as to face myself and learn the depths of Your love.
For it is in being uncertain and not in control that we find true faith,
in knowing the limits of mind and body that we find wholeness of Spirit,
and in passing through death that we find life everlasting.
Amen.
—Author: Judith Kubish

* **Prayer to remove negativity:** Sometimes we become convinced that we cannot improve ourselves or our lives. We need to remember that God can do what no human power can. Pray for God to help you remove those limiting beliefs that have become barriers to you becoming all that God wants you to be.

If you want to add visualization to your prayer, when you inhale, breathe in God's strength. Imagine God's power flowing through your brain like a strong wind blowing down all of the limiting walls which you have accepted as real and which are blocking you from reaching your potential. Imagine those walls being reduced to rubble and ashes. When you exhale, breathe out the dust and debris that are left behind, as God sweeps your mind clear of your limiting misconceptions.

* **Cleansing prayers:** Starting your day with a cleansing morning meditation can give you a fresh start to the day.

Ask God to purify your mind and your heart and remove your emotional baggage. Visualize God's love entering you from above, swirling around, scrubbing away the garbage—first in your mind, then sinking down and cleansing your heart, then lowering further and clearing away all of the tension and emotional garbage you have been carrying in your "guts." Finally, imagine all of that cleared negativity leaving your body through your feet. Repeat the process, letting God's energy fill you and flush out the garbage, over and over again. This meditation can help release tension that you aren't even aware that you are carrying around.

In the book *Twelve Steps and Twelve Traditions*, it states that good results can be achieved if we combine self-examination (steps 4, 5, and 10), meditation, and prayer.[17] You can ask God to remove a specific character defect that you have identified in your step work. To add visualization, breathe in God's goodness and grace then breathe out your character defects.

If you don't have a specific character defect you want God to remove, you can ask Him to cleanse you and remove any preconceived ideas and prior programming that may be preventing you from having a better experience with God and with yourself. Each time you inhale, breathe in God's love and power. When you exhale, release the negative garbage that you have collected throughout your life, which limits you from fulfilling your purpose and being an effective tool in God's hands.

You can also use visualizations without prayers attached. During these meditations, you are not asking something of God; you simply focus on being open to receive whatever God wants to give you. Perhaps visualize an opening at the top of your head, and imagine God's will entering your mind and directing your thoughts.

★ **Breathe in God's grace; breathe out God's love.** God's grace cannot be earned; it is freely given. When you receive God's grace, you practice being able to receive all of the blessings that God wants to give you, whether you feel that you deserve them or not. When you inhale, imagine God's grace as a golden light, or warmth, flowing into you.

As you breathe out God's love, imagine yourself becoming surrounded by a thickening cloud of God's love. This will act as a buffer between you and other people.

Throughout the day, everything anyone says or does toward you has to pass through a cloud of God's love, which transforms everything, before it impacts you. Also, everything you say or do toward others has to pass through God's love before it affects them.

I do this meditation especially on days when I think it might be useful to have "the armor of God's love" around me, protecting me throughout the day.

★ **Breathe in gratitude; breathe out joy.** After your prayer time, spend a few minutes writing a list of things for which you are grateful. Repeatedly inhale your gratitude for being blessed; exhale the happiness you feel to have such a blessed life. Focusing on the good things in your life creates positive energy, which you can then share with others. Negative thoughts create a negative life. Positive thoughts create a positive life. Do the footwork to get the life you want.

Later, you can use any of the items on your gratitude list as the basis for a separate meditation. This will help you focus on being aware of how good your life is.

★ Breathe in peace; breathe out tension and pain. When I'm dealing with stressful or painful situations, I like to visualize myself being held in God's hands. This visualization might work for you. Alternatively, you could imagine God standing next to you, with His arm around your shoulders, etc.

Picture yourself experiencing whatever intimate connection with God that will bring you comfort. When you breathe in, think of receiving God's loving care, compassion, and soothing comfort. Set your mind to experience a sense of peaceful calm growing within you, every time you inhale. When you exhale, imagine all of the accumulated tension and negative energy leaving your body. Imagine all traces of your problems, and your negative reactions to those problems, fading away as you turn them over to God.

★ Filling with God's Love. Ask God to fill you with His love, so that you can be a channel for His love throughout the day. You can't give away what you don't have. If you spend time filling with God's love in the morning, you will have a full supply of love to share with others. Throughout the day, share the feeling of being loved and being full of love with the people you encounter.

Perhaps visualize luxuriating in a comfortable, warm bathtub—soaking God's love into every pore—expanding with God's love like a sponge. Alternatively, imagine yourself, or your heart, opening up to God. Perhaps picture your heart as a flower, and watch the petals unfold. Now imagine God dripping whatever you need down in between the petals of your heart-flower—love, happiness, serenity, etc.—like sunshine and rain nourish real flowers. As you go through your day, imagine offering yourself as a beautifully nurtured flower to everyone you meet.

★ **Send love and healing energy to others**. After you have opened your mind and heart to God, think of someone who would benefit from receiving God's love and healing power. Focus on that individual as you receive God's love and strength. Imagine yourself being a channel for the energy you receive from God, and send it out to the person you are holding in your thoughts. Imagine beams of loving energy flowing into you from God, then extending from you to the other person.

Inspirational authors: You can find good topics for your meditations in spiritual literature, such as books written by Emmet Fox and Melody Beattie, etc. One of the many books that have a different inspirational thought for each day of the year can also be used as the basis for meditations. As previously mentioned, when using a spiritual book as the inspiration for your meditations, check to be sure that the thoughts and ideas presented are in line with your Twelve Step program.

After meditating for a while on your chosen idea, set aside some time to just sit and reflect on your connection with God and what God might want to communicate to you, then start writing what you "hear."

The format for your prayer and meditation session is: *pray, read, meditate, write,* and *share.*

As you practice meditating, your own ideas for good meditations will occur to you. Try your mediation ideas, and when you find something that inspires you, list it in your meditation journal as a subject for further reflection.

There are no limits to what you can do, or how far you can go, in your meditation practice. That is because in meditation, we connect with God, and God has infinite power. It excites me to know that there are no limitations to my meditation adventure!

CHAPTER 12

IF YOU EXPERIENCE
DIFFICULTY MEDITATING

Sometimes I have "dry" days, where I don't seem to get any valuable messages regarding what God's will is for me during my meditation time. That is to be expected. Meditation experiences vary. Sometimes I just get a list of things to do or people to pray for, but other times I get thoughts and ideas that resonate deeply within me, and open my eyes to a new perspective and/or a better approach to a situation. Open your mind and heart to receive whatever God decides to give you each time you pray and meditate. As you spend time developing this practice, your relationship with God will become stronger.

Simply spending time in the presence of God is a beautiful meditation experience, even if you were seeking direction regarding a particular problem. A solution to your problem may occur at a later time, in God's time. Developing your relationship with God should be your primary goal, not getting answers to your questions or problems.

If you repeatedly have difficulty meditating, similar to what authors refer to as "writer's block," it may be an indication that you need to work through something that is blocking your meditation practice. Here is a list of the more frequently mentioned blocks to meditation, followed by some suggestions on how to deal with them:

- problems with your concept of God
- expectations
- distractions
- pressure to perform
- baggage
- resentments
- feeling unworthy
- not following instructions
- fear of making mistakes

Problems with your concept of God: Many people who come into Twelve Step programs have an unpleasant, or uncomfortable, concept of God. Some have had bad experiences with a particular religion or childhood church experiences and developed a mental block about "that God thing."

Someone I know had developed a negative mind-set toward God, due to extremely difficult childhood experiences. She told me, "If there was a 'loving God,' He wouldn't have let those things happen to me when I was a girl!" In order to get past that block, she had to create a simple concept of God. "God is good. Good is God. If it isn't good, it isn't from God." That opened her mind and heart to receive what God has to offer her.

A childhood friend of mine was raised as an atheist. When he started working a Twelve Step program, he didn't know how he could possibly do Steps 2 and 3. He thought it was going to be impossible to develop a belief in a Higher Power and then learn to trust that Higher Power for guidance and direction.

His sponsor told my friend, "Fake it until you can make it. Do what it says in the book *Alcoholics Anonymous*: create your own concept of God, and pray to him every morning and every night. Do that for a month, and see what happens."

My friend followed this direction and discovered that the days when he prayed were a lot better than the days when he got out of bed and started his day without his morning prayer and quiet time. My friend later reported, "I don't know what God is. I don't think my brain is big enough to be able to understand what God is. I just now know that God exists—and that prayer and meditation work." (This friend has many years of sobriety today.)

Open your mind to accept a new concept of God, and embrace the opportunity to create a new relationship with God as He appears in your life today.

Twelve Step literature states that having an open mind is all that is required to begin having a spiritual experience. Spiritual experiences come in all shapes and sizes. Your understanding of how God can appear in, and can guide your life, will develop and enlarge over time. Just try to be willing to accept the possibility of a power greater than yourself. That will open the door for your first awareness of God's presence. Keep your mind open, and God will be able to teach you more and more about what He wants for your life.

Expectations: I found it very helpful to set aside all of my preconceived ideas about prayer and meditation, and my thoughts about how God "should" communicate with me.

(No chorus of angels' harps has ever accompanied one of my meditation "messages.") I didn't expect to receive visual images as communications, but meaningful mental pictures often occur during my meditation sessions, which clearly speak to me.

I decided to set aside all of my expectations and let God use whatever channel He wanted to use, to broadcast His messages to me. That has been working quite well, almost every day, since November 2010.

Meditation experiences vary. I suggest you approach each meditation as if you were opening a gift and just be willing to receive whatever God gives you each time. Think of it like opening birthday presents; it's exciting not to know what each wrapped present is going to turn out to be. Receive and appreciate each one as it appears.

If you judge your meditation experience as "not really that good" or "not working," you may become discouraged. Don't give up before the gifts start appearing. Persist. Try changing where or when you meditate. Try meditating with someone else. Be creative and try other possible solutions.

Even after you have established the pattern of daily meditation, you can have days where it's difficult to find time to meditate or to get good results. It can seem impossible to be disciplined about focusing on what God is trying to communicate to you on holidays and vacations, when you have company, when someone in the house is sick and you have care-taking duties added to your schedule, etc.

Don't focus on, or beat yourself up for, the "missed" days. Just accept that day's experience for what it is, and wait to try again next time.

Distractions: When random thoughts interrupt your meditation process, don't start judging how poorly you are doing or how undisciplined your brain is. Judgment is another distraction. Whenever you notice that your mind has wandered, simply return your mind to a point of focus (such as your breath) and start again.

Try to let passing thoughts drift through your mind. Imagine each thought is like a car; rather than getting into one of the cars and going for a ride (letting it take you away from your meditation practice), choose to just stand on the street corner and watch the traffic go by. Say to yourself, "There goes another thought."

When this doesn't work, accept that it is human nature to have an active mind. Instead of fixating on how much your mind wanders, focus on the positive. Applaud yourself for becoming aware that you had left your meditation practice, and then bring yourself back to a point of focus.

If you keep having a persistent thought about something you should take care of, rather than letting it continue to disrupt your meditation, just make a note about it (so you can deal with it later) and return to your meditation. Get back into your connection with God by asking what His will is for you today or what He wants to say to you right now. God's will isn't for you to fail, to feel frustrated, or to waste time in self-criticism about not staying focused. God has better plans for you!

You might try listening to some calming music while you meditate, or try doing some yoga (or other stretching, centering exercise) before you meditate, to help focus your mind. Experiment and play around with different ideas, until you find what works best for you.

Pressure to perform: I share my daily meditations with several people. There were times when I wasn't hearing anything regarding God's will for me and I found myself telling God, "Hey, I have people waiting to hear my message today. Give me something!" If I stopped and shifted my focus onto God, and onto what God wanted to say to me, I got better reception.

Focusing on God, instead of trying to satisfy your (or anyone else's) requirements, forms a strong connection between you and God. God is the author of your meditation experience; listen for His words.

Any time you find yourself focusing on what you want to get out of your meditation, you can stop and re-center yourself by focusing on breathing in God's love and breathing out peace. Do this as often as necessary.

Baggage: I learned a clearing exercise at the first prayer and meditation retreat I attended. You may find it helpful to go through this "backpack" visualization before you meditate. Think of everything you carry around in the back of your mind, or in the deepest part of your heart, as baggage. This also applies to those nagging to-do lists, which can be so distracting during meditation.

The weight you are carrying around in your backpack includes everything you worry about, all your plans and wishes, frustrated dreams, financial fears, irritations at neighbors and coworkers, and those things that you never find time to do. Think of how heavy a load you are carrying throughout your day, every day, perhaps without even being aware of most of it. How tiring that can be!

Before you start meditating, imagine taking off your backpack. Really focus on how that would feel, as you remove one strap at a time. Feel the weight transfer off of your shoulders as you let your backpack slip down into your hands, and then onto the floor. Give your backpack of concerns into God's hands.

Now you have room to receive whatever God wants to give you during your meditation experience, because you're not already carrying a fully loaded backpack. (It's there for you to pick up again, whenever you want it back.)

Because this "backpack" exercise focuses your attention, it helps clear your mind of distractions, which sets the stage for a better meditation experience.

Resentments: Carrying a resentment is like carrying old food around in your backpack. After a while, it can really start to stink! Forgiveness is an emotional housecleaning of the old, "stinky stuff" that you've been packing around for too long, which can't be put to any good purpose.

Forgiveness is a decision and an action, not an emotion. In some cases, usually when someone I love is hurt, I just can't make myself feel forgiveness. I was told that I should choose to forgive and take the action of forgiveness. I can make an agreement with God that I am choosing to forgive someone— stating the date and the time I agree to forgive that person. Feeling free of resentment will follow my taking that action (sometimes quickly, sometimes slowly), but I will have taken the action of forgiveness.

Sometimes I discover bits and pieces of old resentments tucked in the corners at the bottom of my backpack, which didn't get cleared out during my forgiveness process, and I have to do the exercise again. I've found that forgiveness is like a muscle—the more I use it, the better I get at it and the more I can do with it. The more I clean out my backpack, the better I feel, and the more good energy I have to share with others.

You might want to do a forgiveness exercise. Set aside some time to sit down with a pen and paper and make a thorough list of everything you feel someone or some institution owes you—every "debt" which you haven't canceled. When you have a complete list, place your hand on top of it and pray a version of the below prayer.

Forgiveness Prayer

God, I don't want anything or anyone—past or present—to keep me from having a good, strong, and intimate experience with you. Therefore, I am deciding to forgive all of the people (or institutions) on this list, whether I feel like it or not. I am deciding to cancel all of their debts right now.
Amen.

People have found that "date stamping" when they do this forgiveness exercise helps seal the deal in their minds. If they record the date and time, issues regarding old baggage resurface much less often. Write down when you make your decision to forgive. Then let go, and let God carry that burden from that point forward. (You might want to put this list of resentments in your "God box.")

Feeling unworthy: I once started a mediation session with asking God to help me feel closer to Him. During that mediation, I remembered the last time I drove drunk and risked hurting someone. During my meditation, I heard that I needed to let myself fully receive God's forgiveness. I also heard that in order to accept God's forgiveness, I had to fully forgive myself.

God had already forgiven me. I was told to forgive myself, to remove blocks between God and me.

If you notice that you're feeling bad about something you've done, said, or thought, you can do a forgiveness meditation on yourself. Ask for God's forgiveness for anything that is making you feel guilty. Then let yourself receive God's forgiveness. Possibly pray, "God, I receive your forgiveness for _____ (fill in the blank) today, and I now choose to forgive myself." Record the date and time.

During this meditation, *breathe in forgiveness*, imagining God's forgiveness entering into and swirling through your brain, your heart, and your "guts"—clearing out all of the old issues you're holding in storage. Then *breathe out peace*, imagining all of the old garbage you've been packing around leaving with every breath you exhale—and feeling an increasing sense of well-being.

While you focus on feeling forgiven and peaceful, listen for what God might be trying to say to you. Move forward in your newly cleansed relationship with God.

Not following God's instructions: When meditating to learn God's will for you, it's important to follow any directions you receive. It negatively affects my relationships with others if it doesn't seem that what I say matters to them, or when people don't seem to listen to me. Eventually, I decide there's no reason to try to communicate. I don't want God to feel that way about me.

I think that having a good relationship with God takes as much work and commitment as maintaining good relationships with our family and friends. Respect and love are the basis for a good relationship. Respect the messages you receive in meditation. If you want direction on how to have a good life, it makes sense to follow the directions you receive. Refusing to do God's will is a block to having good meditation experiences.

A speaker at the 50th Annual Women's International AA Conference said that in the early days of AA, when people did the first part of Step 11 (which tells you that before you go to sleep, you should think back over your actions of the day), that "review" process included going over the list of instructions which were received in morning meditation and verifying that any directions you received for that day had been followed.

As part of your nightly review, check to be sure that you took care of everything you were directed to do in your morning meditation. If you realize that you didn't do something God instructed you to do, apologize. Ask for God's forgiveness, accept His forgiveness, and then make plans to set things right.

You can start over with God any time you choose to do so, but setting things right with God at the close of each day, as instructed in Step 11 of the book *Alcoholics Anonymous*, will help you sleep with a clear mind and heart. Then you will awaken feeling more refreshed, and with a clean slate, as you start your new day.

Fear of making mistakes: You shouldn't expect to do everything perfectly, especially while you are learning. At first, it can be difficult to believe that you are getting messages from God. You may wonder if the thoughts you get during meditation are just something you created.

If you are unsure that something really is God's will, take time to pray and meditate on the same subject again, until the correct action becomes clear to you.

Sometimes the ideas you get in meditation can start out very small, like a seed, and they are difficult to understand. As you continue meditating on them, these thoughts can develop and change until a clear picture comes into focus. Your ability to get clear reception, and to discern the difference between God's thoughts and your ideas, will improve over time.

One way to avoid mistakes is to stay open to making modifications to your original thought. In one of my meditations, I heard, "As you prepare your plans for the day, be sure to work in pencil, and remember that God has an eraser in His hand." Be open to receive God's input, and change your plans to align with God's will, as it is revealed to you over time.

You can test any thought you get in meditation by asking if it is based in love. Everything from God is based in love. Messages from God will be your highest thoughts. Another test is to ask if what you heard is free of self-motivated interest. Try to rid yourself of wrong motives and self-will, and then open yourself to hear God's answers to your questions.

Sometimes, it makes sense to pause and confirm before following the directions you thought God gave you. This is especially true as you are beginning to develop a meditation practice, while you are learning to clearly recognize God's voice. In these cases, discuss the message you received in meditation with someone you trust, preferably someone who understands the principles of your Twelve Step program and participates in two-way communication with God (possibly your sponsor).

While you attempt to remove the blocks you have encountered in your meditation practice, remember that you are not working alone. Pray for, and receive, God's help in removing your blocks. Then keep suiting up, showing up, and doing your best. God wants to have a close relationship with you; it will come to pass, if you pray for it and work with God to achieve it. As it says in *Alcoholics Anonymous*, "God can remove whatever self-will has blocked you off from Him."[18]

As your prayer and meditation practice develops, you will probably have better and better experiences. Register how those "good" meditations feel. During future meditation sessions, those memories can help you have similar experiences. If you focus on what it feels like to be in the presence of God, it makes it easier to establish that connection again.

CHAPTER 13

POWERFUL LESSONS

I have a very vivid memory of my near-death experience in 1984. I went someplace where I felt God. (I didn't "see" an image of God, but I felt God's presence.) There was unlimited love and harmony that extended throughout all things and all time. I do not have the vocabulary to accurately describe that feeling of no limitations on distance and time; *infinity* and *forever* don't come close to encompassing the vastness of the experience. Trying to describe the feeling of God's presence is even more difficult to put into words.

While I was out there (wherever that was), I clearly received a message. "Everything is the way it's supposed to be, always and forever." That created a feeling of deep and boundless peace.

At the exact moment when I was getting that message, my father (who was holding my hand in the hospital room) said, "Cathy, we can't tell if you're still with us. If you can hear my voice, squeeze my hand." I felt so disappointed when I heard those words! I wanted to cross over into that amazing place which I was close to entering. I wanted to become part of what

I refer to now as "The All." But I was raised to be obedient to parental authority, so I turned around and came back. I remember thinking, *Oh no, I have to go back to that room and the pain!*

When I was told by the doctors that I was so brain injured that I would never again be employable, that I'd lost the use of one hand and one leg, and that my fiancé had died in the accident, it was hard not to believe my condition was hopeless. I continually reminded myself that God had everything under control; that everything was exactly the way it was supposed to be. That helped me accept my broken condition.

The knowledge that a loving God was in control got me through months of doctors' appointments and physical therapy sessions, without experiencing improvement. I don't think I could have continued to "suit up and show up" day after day, if I hadn't had that idea to hold onto. And I did finally experience a successful recovery, because I had faith and I consistently followed directions. That experience taught me that applying the principles of my Twelve Step program in other areas of my life *does* work.

Over the years, focusing on the thought that God has everything under control has helped me accept many situations I don't really like. I know that I don't have the ability to see what God is creating or to understand why things have to be a certain way. Understanding and approval aren't requirements for acceptance—just faith that God knows what He is doing.

When you pray and meditate, you are connecting with the power that is painting the "big picture," and that is the source of all knowledge. When you ask for the knowledge of God's will for you, you are asking how you can participate harmoniously in God's creation. That's an exciting undertaking!

I learned another incredible lesson at an AA convention in Seaside, Oregon. To close the convention, Rona Y. performed the song "Amazing Grace." I was stunned as I listened to her, because I recognized the feeling of God in the room. I experienced the same feeling I had encountered during my near-death experience.

I learned in that convention hall that it is possible to feel God's presence *here and now.* I had previously thought that you had to die, or nearly die, to be able to feel God's presence. That was an amazing new insight!

That awareness inspired me to discover how to connect and communicate with God on a daily basis, as it is outlined in Step 11 in the book *Alcoholics Anonymous.*

In meditation, I can recreate what it felt like to be in God's presence. Some days that doesn't happen fully, especially on those mornings when I feel a need to rush through my mediation, because I have so many "important" things to do. However, during some meditations, I feel a very strong connection to God.

It's easy to forget what's really important, when you get caught up with the requirements of day-to-day living.

Being aware of God's presence in your life, and of God's will for you, is really the most important thing you can do. God wants the absolute best for you. If you listen for, and follow His guidance, you can work with God to create a life that is happier and more meaningful. You will also become more capable of uplifting others.

What could be more important than experiencing a strong enough connection to God that you receive messages on how to live a more purposeful and fulfilling life? What do you have on your list of things to do that's more important than receiving a personal message from the Creator of the Universe? If you stop to ask yourself those questions, I believe it will reinforce the fact that you should consistently prioritize making time in your daily schedule for the life-enhancing practice of prayer and meditation.

CHAPTER 14

THE TRANSFORMING POWER
OF MEDITATION

At first, meditation was just one more item on my list of things to do, but as I continue with my daily sessions, the time I spend in meditation has become a favorite time of day. Now I absolutely love soaking in God's presence and feeling my connection to my Higher Power.

I've found that my relationship with God has developed over time, similar to the way most relationships progress. At first it seemed awkward, and I preferred to have a planned activity or agenda or to follow, like when you first start dating someone. But after our relationship deepened, due to spending a significant amount of quality time together, I found myself being able to enjoy just being in God's presence.

When I first started meditating, it was helpful to have a phrase or spiritual reading to use as the focus for my meditation. I needed to have a subject, or topic, to bring to my conversation with God. I have found that over time, it has become much easier to just sit silently in God's presence, awaiting any communication that may occur.

The practice of consistent meditation has created significant beneficial changes within me. Every morning, I try to set myself (my agenda and my ego) aside and invite God in to direct my plans for the day. That is a very clear pathway to improvement!

The messages I get during meditation help me become aware of, and correct, harmful old patterns of behavior. I often get ideas regarding different ways to approach old problems, versus continuing to use my old ways of thinking and letting bad habits recreate the same problem again and again.

Sometimes I discover that I'm holding onto anger or resentments, without being aware of it. If I pray and meditate about the problem, I often get thoughts about how to change my perspective, to process and release negative feelings.

I also get meditation messages about how to avoid letting my defects of character negatively affect my relationships. Prayer and meditation have helped me improve my existing relationships and have helped me form many more enjoyable, valuable relationships. My circle of friends has expanded to include a great number of amazingly loving and supportive people.

Prayer and meditation help me be calmer and more accepting of whatever is going on in life. My family began to notice the difference that practicing prayer and meditation was making in me, even before I was aware of it. Before I developed my meditation practice, I had no emotional sobriety and would often lose my temper and yell at my loved ones. When meditation became part of my daily routine, I became a much calmer and more pleasant person to be around.

In meditation, I hear that acceptance is the answer to all of my problems. This helps me eliminate expectations (which can develop into resentments, if they are not met). I have learned through experience that God will give me whatever I need to take care of the things that He wants me to accomplish, so I can be more relaxed now. As a result, I don't have such a need to control things, to make things go the way I think they should.

Because I'm more open and flexible, the amount of anger and frustration I experience is greatly reduced. Before I started daily prayer and meditation, I felt a need to know exactly how things were going to happen, so that I could be prepared and feel secure. If things didn't go the way I had envisioned, I experienced frustration, anger, or fear. Those emotions could take over and ruin whole days.

Today, I try not to let unpleasant emotions waste any more of my life, because God keeps showing me that I have better things to do with my time and energy.

CHAPTER 15

OBSERVATIONS FROM OTHERS

The following are statements from some significant people in my life, regarding the changes they have noticed since I started my daily practice of prayer and meditation.

> I met Cathy back in May of 1996, when she first came into the program. She was outgoing, to say the least! Her nickname was "Crazy Cathy," and she seemed to need to get attention and validation from other people all of the time. Over the years, there has been steady growth, but nothing like what I have seen since she began to pray and meditate daily. The change I have seen in Cathy is really too big for words. She has been "rocketed into the fourth dimension," like it says in the book *Alcoholics Anonymous*.
>
> She now is working for improvement and changes from the inside out and has been gracious enough to share her experience,

strength, and hope with many of us. She no longer needs to get attention and validation from outside of herself; she is getting it daily from God. The peace and serenity Cathy exude are infectious!

—Joann M., my sponsor, twenty-three years sober

I've known Cathy for sixteen years, and she is one of my very best friends. When we first met, she was scary! She was tough, standoffish, and slightly aggressive. Today I find her to be one of the most inspirational women I have ever met, not only because of her survival story, but her seemingly fearless approach to self-study, growth, and the maintenance of her spiritual condition. Over the years she has softened in attitude and approach to life, but underneath, there was still the unsettled, unsatisfied girl who wasn't quite comfortable with herself.

In the last five years, I have seen an *amazing* change in my friend Cathy ... since she has been dedicated to meditation and getting quiet with God. I see in her softness and beauty that has always been there but did not shine as it does today! You not only see the difference in her, you can feel that the energy around her is much more relaxed and joyful.

Cathy is compassionate, loving, and truly a gift to those who encounter her. Today I see her tackle situations that used to baffle her, with grace and love in her heart. She still has all that great energy that way back in the day sort of scared me, but today it is funneled into goodness, acceptance, peace, and enjoying the moment! She truly is a wonderful example of working a good recovery program and living each day to the fullest.

—Dana K., my long-time AA friend, twenty years sober

I reconnected with Cathy after she had done a prayer and meditation workshop with Tom. I saw this beautiful, gracious woman who was becoming very spiritual, and I wanted what she had. It was then that I asked her to again be my sponsor.

I know that, initially, meditation was not an easy process for her. I saw her willingness and her determination. I continue to watch her spiritual graciousness, and it has in a beautiful way impacted my own recovery. I have recently attended a prayer and meditation workshop with her, and she continues to guide me with her wisdom and knowledge. Because of that, there has been a shift for me in my life as I move forward on my spiritual journey. I will be forever grateful to Cathy for this gift.

—Terri Y., my sponsee, fourteen years sober

Before she started practicing daily meditation, Cathy was always moving around. She couldn't really sit still and just enjoy one thing; she always felt the need to be doing one or two other tasks simultaneously. She was stressed most of the time. New tasks being added onto her workload would spike her anxiety level, and this upset her relationships with other people.

The more Cathy practiced daily meditation and shared what she got during those meditations with others, the better she got at handling life's bumps and sharp turns. She got into gardening, could sit and watch birds enjoy her garden, and she got back into reading for pleasure (something she hadn't been able to do for years).

What's more impressive than just her own improvement in handling stress and her understanding of her own limitations and past issues, is that when she shares her meditations with others, it helps them work on their problems. This doesn't just occur in her meditations groups; she has also helped people who do not have their own meditation practice.

Her increased ability to work through emotional turmoil and her increased peace of mind have made her a better ally to her friends (helping them with their troubles) and have made her an even better role model for her son.

—Steven J., my son

CHAPTER 16

SHARE YOUR MEDITATION JOURNEY

While I was doing my "ninety meditations in ninety days," after my first prayer and meditation retreat, more and more people started noticing a difference in me. People who had known me for quite a while started asking me what I was doing differently, that had changed me so much. (This was after fourteen years of sobriety. The change was that noticeable!) Recently my sponsor said,

> I wish that the newcomers who hear you share in the rooms today could have heard you speak even a few months ago, so they could get perspective on how different you are today. You're not the same person now! People should know that it's possible to change this much.

I started explaining to people about my experiences learning to meditate. Several people were so impressed by the difference they saw in me that they wanted to be included in my shared meditations, so I began sharing with others the daily meditation messages that I sent my prayer and meditation buddy every day. Over the last few years, I have texted or emailed my daily meditations to an average of twenty people every day. Some of these people have gone on to form their own prayer and meditation groups.

For many people, it helps to have a group, to keep them accountable and dedicated to the practice of daily prayer and meditation. This may help you, or you could do this to help others.

Members of groups who meet in person sometimes experience a shared meditation. This only occurs when people meditate in the same place. Frequently many members of the group get variations of the same message, which is an interesting and inspiring process.

You might want to consider starting group prayer and meditation sessions in your community. Alternatively, many of us (who have difficulty meeting together in a place that is mutually convenient) enjoy being connected via cell phone or email. Decide what works for you.

Many of the people I had on my original contact list, for daily meditation messages, have attended prayer and meditation workshops in my home. Several people who attended these workshops have remarked that what they learned in the workshops helped them improve their conscious contact with the God of their understanding and that they are now living happier and more rewarding lives.

You might develop your meditation practice to the point where you do Step 11 calls, reaching out to others to share what you know about prayer and meditation.

CHAPTER 17

SUMMARY

The process that Tom R. outlines in his book *Prayer & Meditation: A Practical Guide to the Promises Found in Step 11* really works. If "Crazy Cathy" can go from not being able to meditate at all to meditating on a daily basis for years—and watching my personality, my relationships, and my life change for the better—so can everyone.

In the book titled *Twelve Steps and Twelve Traditions*, it states,

> Meditation is something which can always be further developed. It has no boundaries, either in width or height. Aided by such instruction and example as we can find, it is essentially an individual adventure, something which each one of us works out in his own way.[19]

This book is my example of how I am using the instruction I received from Tom R., along with what it says about prayer and meditation in our Twelve Step literature, to develop an enjoyable and effective daily Step 11 routine. I sincerely hope that my story helps inspire you to expand your prayer and meditation practice.

Please don't let yourself get trapped into believing that you have to have one certain kind of meditation experience in order for it to be a "good" practice. Your meditation adventure is an individual experience, one that you can develop in your own way.

Find a time and a place that works for you, and schedule time every day to work on developing your relationship with your Higher Power. Setting time aside to focus on anyone will improve that relationship. It only makes sense to invest consistent time in improving your relationship with God.

Like learning to play the piano, it takes time and practice to consistently get good results, but I have found that the benefits are very much worth the effort.

God wants the absolute best for you. God wants to help you become a better and happier person. God wants your relationship with Him to be a good one. God wants to be able to communicate with you, to help you improve your life; He wants to be understood. Stay with your prayer and meditation practice long enough that it has a chance to develop.

Whenever life gets hectic, remember that God can restore you to a state of calm, if He is sought. God is always as close as your next quiet time. Whenever you want to feel close to God, simply take a few minutes and practice a focused meditation. God will appear, to those who seek.

My life has been greatly transformed for the better, through my prayer and meditation practice, and it is continuing to improve. You can also use prayer and meditation to partner with God and create a life beyond your wildest dreams. What are you waiting for?

PART 3
SAMPLE MEDITATIONS

MY FIRST "NINETY IN NINETY" MEDITATIONS

As you begin your daily prayer and meditation practice, working with a partner will help you be more disciplined. Ask someone to commit with you to doing ninety prayer and meditation sessions in ninety days. I did this after my first Step 11 workshop, and it was very helpful.

My partner and I agreed that for ninety days we would both pray and meditate, then exchange with each other what we got out of our meditation session that day—by phone, text message, or email. This was to help us establish the discipline of daily prayer and meditation. It worked.

I continued to pray and meditate daily from that point forward and kept journals of what I experienced. I didn't miss one day for over two years, and I still rarely miss a day, because I so completely enjoy all of the positive benefits I have realized through practicing prayer and meditation.

The following are my first "ninety in ninety" meditation messages. These are my actual first ninety days' meditations;

they aren't selected "good" messages. This is a real example of what you can experience as you work Step 11.

Day #1, 11/15/10
Meditation: Feel God's love soaking into you.

Fill with God's love, so that love will be your energy source for this day. Remember to keep turning your day over to God. Throughout the day, you can pause and say, "God's will, not mine." If it's God's will, it will have love as its source.

Positive intention for the day: Feel peaceful and centered in love. Act from that loving center.

Day #2, 11/16/2010
Meditation: Ask God to guide your day.

When I did this meditation, I got a visual of a broom sweeping junk away. I heard to stop spending time and energy on unimportant stuff. I need to sweep other people's stuff out of my life, too. I need to stop letting other people's negative junk affect my mind and heart negatively.

Focus on the positive things in your life. Don't let little mistakes distract you from the main focus of your journey, which is to become the person God created you to be.

Positive intention for the day: Feel God's love. Find God's will. Share God's blessings.

Day #3, 11/17/2010
Meditation: Be a source of God's good energy.

React from your heart, not from your head. Look for the good, focus on the good, and good will direct your path. Focus on God, instead of getting distracted by your ego.

Ask for God's will continuously, especially when faced with distraction or conflict.

Positive intention for the day: Put God in front of you as you go through your day. Like the pointed prow of a boat, having God in front of you will smoothly part the waters through which you travel. You will meet with less resistance and create less turbulence than when your ego leads the way.

Day #4, 11/18/2010
Meditation: Slow down and enjoy each moment of your day.

God wants you to enjoy your journey. Take time to become aware of the blessings and the goodness around you. Enjoy *now*, one *now* at a time.

Inhale God's grace. Let His essence saturate your entire being. Exhale God's love, so that it affects everything around you. Seeing the world through a layer of God's love will change how you perceive things, like looking through a new pair of glasses.

Positive intention for the day: Don't try to change others. Focus on surrounding yourself with a protective bubble of God's love and grace.

Day #5, 11/19/2010
Meditation: Improving yourself improves your relationships.

During this meditation, I saw a comparison between my soul and a garden.

Prepare the soil of your soul's garden every day—locating and removing the weeds (character defects) and watering the earth with loving care (prayer and meditation). That will help the seeds that God plants take root and grow into good qualities, and others can enjoy the results of you having a more beautiful spirit.

Positive intention for the day: Add to the beauty of God's world.

Day #6, 11/20/2010
Meditation: God knows much better than you exactly what you need and what you don't need. Also, your loving God wants what is best for you. Let go; let God.

God put you right where you are, right now. You are right where you're supposed to be at this moment in time. Relax and enjoy your present circumstances. Doing God's will is much easier than trying to control everything. Just ask for the next indicated step.

Take down the barriers and walls around you, and connect with God. Look for signs of God's direction. Fill your present moment with God's love, and allow that to flow through you to others. That is always God's will for you. When in doubt, focus on being a channel for God's love.

Positive intention for the day: Give away the good energy you receive from God.

Day #7, 11/21/2010
Meditation: Your present circumstances are a brief moment in time.

God's will is like a river of love. Stop struggling and just go with the mighty flow of God's will. I got the mental picture of someone in a large body of water, struggling in fear of drowning. If that person relaxes and lies back, 99 percent of the time he will float with his nose, eyes, and mouth above water level. What he was afraid of will actually support him, if he stops struggling and relaxes.

Positive intention for the day: Relax and trust God to support you as this moment and your present circumstances pass by, in God's time.

Day #8, 11/22/2010
Meditation: God loves us all. Breathe in God's love, and then share it with others.

The most important thing in all relationships is love. If you want to receive unconditional love and acceptance, you also need to give it to others. Self-help books focus on boundaries and self-care, and that's part of relationships. But God wants you to shift your focus from emotional survival to expressing God's love to others.

Positive intention for the day: Be sure that your "in" valve is always set in the open position to receive God's love. When you have what you need, then you can channel it to others.

Day #9, 11/23/2010
Meditation: God's love heals. God is healing you, in all ways, one day at a time.

I was taught to pray, "God, heal me in those places where I don't even know that I'm wounded." If you focus on letting God's love soak into you, you can't help but feel better. Then you will be able to act better toward others.

Positive intention for the day: Be aware that all of us have been wounded in some way. Ask yourself what you can do to help heal the people you meet, and interact with, today.

Day #10, 11/24/2010
Meditation: Be aware of God's generous blessings.

Focus on how beautiful life is, and feel gratitude. Enjoy the abundant blessings that God has scattered throughout your life and in the world. God is waiting to give you all of the tools you need to handle any situation that you will encounter today.

Positive intention for the day: Feel confident of God's love. Say thank-you to God for His provisions.

Day #11, 11/25/2010
Meditation: God is meeting your needs.

Accept with grace, serenity, and gratitude all that comes into your life, because God is providing all that you need. Lessons for growth and spiritual development may be hidden in difficult circumstances, and blessings may be waiting for you downstream. Go with the flow, wherever God directs you.

Positive intention for the day: Relax into the arms of God, and have the faith it takes to follow his direction, always. Project your faith in God to those around you.

Day #12, 11/26/2010
Meditation: You are exactly where you're supposed to be, learning the exact lessons you are supposed to be learning at this point in time.

When you are in an uncomfortable place, know that you are being prepared for a change. When things become too uncomfortable to tolerate, the fear of change becomes less important than the pain of continuing. Have faith that God will provide during the transition, when you need to make scary choices to change something.

Positive intention for the day: Live a vibrant life, with personal integrity. Do not compromise your beliefs and standards to please other people. Step out in faith.

Day #13, 11/27/2010
Meditation: God's love is enough.

If you focus on extending God's love to others, you don't have to rely on *your* love being enough. Extend God's forgiving and compassionate love into the universe. God is understanding of our faults and weaknesses and loves us anyway. Try harder to love yourself, and to love others with that same type of love.

Positive intention for the day: Focus on loving God, loving yourself and loving your fellows with unconditional love.

Day # 14, 11/28/2010
Meditation: Turn your will and life over to the care of God.

Stop focusing on the problems and the irritations of daily life. Release your expectations of how it should be. Let it all go, and enjoy this day. God will show you what to do next. Look for and enjoy the good in every situation, instead of wishing it was something other, or something more, than what you are being given.

Positive intention for the day: Instead of focusing on what you want, ask God what you can do for Him today.

Day #15, 11/29/2010
Meditation: Totally enjoy and fully experience your current moment.

Live your life one *now* (second or minute—not hour or day) at a time. Wallow in experiencing your present life and appreciating how blessed you are. You can pray, "Lord, make me an instrument of your peace," but you can't give away what you don't have. Savor the blessings of your *now*, and be fully aware of your connection to God. Others will be able to see and feel the peace you are experiencing from this practice.

Positive intention for the day: Be an example of God's peace.

Day #16, 11/30/2010
Meditation: God wants peace for us all.

I spend a lot of time and energy frantically tying to improve life for myself, and for my family—working on projects, scrambling to find time to fix things, etc. But my life really is beautiful just the way it is. Often solutions to something that bothers me simply unfold while I'm busy struggling uphill on an entirely different path.

Positive intention for the day: Enjoy feeling at peace, and learn to wait in peacefully for a graceful answer.

Day #17, 12/1/2010
Meditation: Taking better care of yourself is a way to say thank-you and send love back to God.

Today I felt God's sadness about how much I push myself and how often I go without enough sleep. I got a comparison of how I feel when my son doesn't eat enough, and I want him to take better care of himself. I wonder if my God feels the same way when I only get five to six hours of sleep a night, over and over again, because I prioritize so many things over taking care of myself.

In meditation, I heard that when I'm stressed about a person or a situation, and my reaction to it, I should pause and ask myself, "How can I send love back to God right now?" instead of "How can I change or fix this?"

Positive intention for the day: Pause throughout the day and say, "God, I love You. What can I do for You right now?"

Day #18, 12/2/2010
Meditation: God is in your life *now*.

When you future-trip, you lose your connection with God. Today, remember to pause and connect with God and celebrate your current moment. God will provide for your needs for each current moment of your life, one *now* at a time.

Positive intention for the day: Be here now. Be as fully present in your current moment as possible, because that is where God is.

Day #19, 12/3/2010
Meditation: Focus on God's unconditional love, His forgiveness, and His grace.

I beat myself up for what are really small mistakes. In meditation, I heard to focus on how completely God forgives each of us, on how abundantly God blesses us, and on how powerfully His grace changes our lives, instead of dwelling on my little mistakes and misfortunes.

Positive intention for the day: Let go of what happened in the past, and live today the best you possibly can. If you feel weak, lean on God's grace to carry you.

Day #20, 12/4/2010
Meditation: I am surrounded with love and support!

Today I was overwhelmed by the awareness of how very blessed I am! God, my family, and my friends are very loving and supportive, even when I make mistakes. When I am in a negative mind-set, I need to open my mind and my heart to become aware of how God's love appears in my life. We are all part of God's family. Feel the bonds.

Positive intention for the day: Focus on loving God always, everywhere, and within everyone you encounter.

Day #21, 12/5/2010
Meditation: Rest in faith that God will provide for all of your needs today.

I'm going through a rough patch of life right now. I recently made some costly mistakes. During meditation this morning, I was reminded of the story in the Bible where God provided daily for His people's needs for food, when manna fell from heaven each day. They were told not to store up food for future consumption, but to trust God to provide each day for that day's needs.

I got the message that God knows precisely what I need to get through just this day, and He has already factored my defects of character into His plan for my day.

Positive intention for the day: All you have to do is walk through today, one step at a time, receiving what God has planned to give you on each step of your journey.

Day #22, 12/6/2010
Meditation: God doesn't want us to live burdened by past mistakes, struggling to move forward. He wants us free to enjoy the blessings He is giving us right now.

Let the river of God's love flow through the collection of regrets, worries, and fears that you are carrying around in your mental "backpack." Let the power of God's love carry your garbage downstream. Choose to release the weight of all of the negative junk you've collected and have chosen to continue packing around.

Positive intention for the day: Turn your focus to God's love and light, and just keep trying to do the best you can in your present moment. Your best is good enough.

Day #23, 12/7/2010
Meditation: Let go; let God.

Let go of your ideas of what you think *should* happen; stop trying to get the results you think *should* occur.

God *always* has the best possible plan. Current events build on past occurrences, and we are all interconnected. You can't know what God is building as you walk through the events of your day. You have to trust that God will create good out of every circumstance—even the situations that appear "bad" at first. Your job is to stop trying to rework or "improve" on God's plan.

Positive intention for the day: Do the best you can, on a continual basis, and leave the "big picture" to God.

Day #24, 12/8/2010
Meditation: You are not alone. Your Higher Power is with you and will always sustain you.

Along with your connection to God, you have the tools of your Twelve Step program, and the fellowship, to help you through difficult times. Everything is doable, with God and with the resources He has brought into your life.

Positive intention for the day: Keep moving through whatever life brings you, knowing that there is a reason for everything—even if you can't see it or know what it is.

Day #25, 12/9/2010
Meditation: Nothing happens in God's world by mistake.

There are lessons to be learned during hard times, and the difficult people we have to deal with provide opportunities for growth. The sunlight of the Spirit, God's love, and God's grace are always waiting to embrace and envelop us. If we have to work through a dark, painful time, the light of God's love is waiting to fill our lives and our hearts with beauty so that we can show the power of God's grace to others.

Positive intention for the day: Be a source of God's light and love in the dark corners you may encounter today.

Day #26, 12/10/2010
Meditation: When you "let go; let God," you are opening yourself to be led by divine guidance.

You have choices regarding what you do and how you respond to guidance. Your choices will lead you either closer to or farther away from God.

If you want to enjoy your day, it makes sense to try to keep God between you and everyone and everything else that you have to deal with today. When you let other people and things get between you and God, you can easily get into trouble. Choose to stay close to God.

Positive intention for the day: Always stay connected to God and be aware of God's presence in your every moment.

Day #27, 12/11/2010
Meditation: Focus on the good and the blessings in your life.

You have a choice to focus on all of the blessings in your life and to create more positive energy. This doesn't mean that you should deny reality, when there are difficulties in your life, just that you shouldn't dwell on the negative and give it more power. Your way of thinking can change your life for the better, or for the worse.

Positive intention for the day: Realize that your thoughts affect your life, positively or negatively. Make good choices regarding what you spend time and energy thinking about, because your thoughts shape and color your life.

Day #28, 12/12/2010
Meditation: God will be sure that you have everything you need to accomplish what He has planned for you today.

If you don't get something you want today, it's because you don't need it to do God's will today. Remember that God wants the absolute best for you. If you want to have a good day, you need to do God's will and stay on the path that He wants you to travel.

Positive intention for the day: Ask for and look for God's direction, then walk through your day, thanking God for providing for your needs.

Day #29, 12/13/2010
Meditation: Be positive and appreciate your present moment. Be aware of and grateful for the blessings in your life.

Write down what you love about your life, and meditate on those things. Make it a goal to have those good things continue and increase in your life. Throughout your day, review your list and confirm that your actions are taking you in the right direction to achieve your goals.

Positive intention for the day: Keep focusing on increasing the good things in your life. Don't allow negative behavior and thoughts to misdirect you.

Day #30, 12/14/2010
Meditation: Choose to focus on the good in your life.

You have the ability to create more good things in your life, by focusing on and improving the good that already exists. Negative thoughts will suddenly appear out of nowhere. Be diligent about not letting your brain entertain those thoughts. Whenever you notice that something negative has come to mind, accept that it is natural for an untrained brain to experience negativity from time to time. Correct the situation by meditating on God's love and the beautiful blessings in your life.

Positive intention for the day: Continually train your brain to entertain positive loving thoughts and to reject negative thoughts as soon as they occur.

Day #31, 12/15/2010
Meditation: God will enrich you, if you allow it, so you will have more to give others. That is God's will.

When you make time to pray and meditate, connecting to God as much as possible, you will fill with spiritually based energy that you can then extend to others. You can only give away that which you already have, so you must fill yourself with God-based thoughts and feelings before you share yourself with others. As you meditate, you are making deposits into your spiritual bank account. With those plentiful reserves, you can give away patience, tolerance, kindness, and love—without running out of supplies.

Positive intention for the day: Soak in God's presence, so His abundant love will become available to others through you, in the cycle of giving and receiving and giving back again.

Day #32, 12/16/2010
Meditation: God wants us all to be happy, joyous, and free.

You can feel, and honor your feelings, without being misled by them. You can talk to others, pray, and meditate, and you can choose to let go of negative feelings. You can practice your Twelve Step program and work toward becoming the person God wants you to be, living the life God wants you to have. Try to not to waste time wallowing in negative feelings and thoughts.

Positive intention for the day: Love is always the answer, especially when it comes to loving yourself. Be kind to yourself. Focus on acceptance, love, and tolerance.

Day #33, 12/17/2010
Meditation: Be aware of the love bonds you have with people today, and appreciate those connections.

We are all children of God. As you meditate and work on becoming the person that God created you to be, the love you feel for others will get stronger. You will grow to feel more gentle and more compassionate and will learn not to push yourself so hard. The more you take care of yourself, the more you will have to offer others.

Positive intention for the day: Look for opportunities to nurture yourself and others. Also, be open to receive nurturing from others.

Day #34, 12/18/2010

Meditation: Be an instrument and a channel for God's grace, peace, and love in this world.

Open yourself to receive grace, peace, and love from God, so you can extend them to others. Meditate with your breath, receiving from God each time you inhale and making room for God's next gift each time you exhale.

- Inhale God's grace; exhale God's peace.
- Inhale God's peace; exhale God's love.
- Inhale God's love; exhale God's grace, creating a bubble of God's grace around you.
- Then inhale God's grace again, and continue the cycle around and around.

Positive intention for the day: Focus on filling yourself with those things you want to pass on to others.

Day #35, 12/19/2010

Meditation: Focus on the positive, so you will be pleasant to be around.

Lots of little things go wrong during the day. You can choose not to let them distract you from the goodness around you and the blessings in your life. When you stay in a positive mind-set, you have good energy to give others, and you are more able to be an instrument of God's peace and love.

Positive intention for the day: Be aware of what you share with others.

Day #36, 12/20/2010
Meditation: Walk through this day in faith.

God is providing for your every need. Live today fully, with your heart and arms fully open to receive God's blessings.

Positive intention for the day: Fully experience today, without the limitations of your own expectations.

Day #37, 12/21/2010
Meditation: Today's prayer was "God, purify my mind."

Relax and know that God is in charge. We are all children of God, and we are all probably doing the best we can. Who am I to judge another's actions and abilities to live their life well? Don't judge. It's hard to love and to judge at the same time. Choose love.

Positive intention for the day: Work on keeping your mind open to see the good in others. Focus on being patient and tolerant, instead of stressed and resentful.

Day #38, 12/22/2010
Meditation: Surrender to God, and He will bless you with exactly what is right and good.

Good things, and good changes, are in God's plan for you. All you have to do is walk in faith until it's God's time for you to receive and experience them, in their perfect time.

Positive intention for the day: Relax and go with the flow of God's plan for your life.

Day #39, 12/23/2010
Meditation: Appreciate the beauty of the world in which you live.

As I looked out the window this morning, I reflected on the amazing miracles that exist in nature. I watched as the sunrise colored the clouds in the sky, and I observed that the grass and roofs all had a thin blanket of frost. I spent time appreciating the blessings that God has woven throughout nature. I got the feeling that it must please God when we take time to appreciate the goodness in our lives.

Positive intention for the day: Focus on the fact that God has provided well for you, that you don't have to worry about how your needs will be met.

Day #40, 12/24/2010
Meditation: Observing nature, we can see similarities between the trees, the flowers, and ourselves.

Recently people have complimented me on the growth they have observed in me during the last few months. Some have said that I am a "blessing" in their lives. That sure wasn't who I was when I started working my Twelve Step program! Maybe like the tree, if I make sure I am firmly rooted in God, and I reach for God's light on a continual basis, I will become stronger and more beautiful as I grow.

Positive intention for the day: Keep reaching for the light; don't spend time in darkness. Strive for growth on a daily basis, trusting in God's plan for your life.

Day #41, 12/25/2010
Meditation: Today's prayer was "God, fill my heart with love, so I can pass it on to others."

Don't spend time and energy thinking about other people's shortcomings or irritating behavior. Don't waste energy thinking about what you want to change in others. Instead, focus on how you can be a better spouse, friend, parent, sibling, coworker, etc.

Positive intention for the day: Focus on improving your side of the street.

Day #42, 12/26/2010
Meditation: God created a beautiful sunrise this morning.

Be aware of the beauty and the blessings that you take for granted. We live in a beautiful world, with miracles all around us! Live in gratitude and appreciation of your blessings today and every day.

Positive intention for the day: Be aware that there are no ordinary days. Each day is full of blessings and has the potential to be amazing!

Day #43, 12/27/2010
Meditation: Today I heard God say, "I am with you."

During tough times, it's hard to feel connected to God, but I am being guided through a time of learning and growth. There is a plan; it is all exactly as it should be. Constant serenity wouldn't promote personal growth.

Positive intention for the day: Look for the lessons, and grow through them.

Day #44, 12/28/2010
Meditation: God is *always* with you, in your heart.

You may need to work on pushing negative thoughts out of your mind. God wants you to focus on the good and to enjoy good relationships. God wants you to feel love and to express love throughout your day.

Positive intention for the day: Work on clearing the garbage from your mind. Focus on living with a heart that is full of God's love.

Day #45, 12/29/2010
Meditation: All you can do is all you can do—and that's all God wants from you.

God doesn't expect or want as much from you as you demand from yourself. You should learn to listen to God's agenda for your day and delete anything that's not in His plans for you.

Positive intention for the day: Take it easy on yourself, look for God's guidance, and be comfortable with His plan for your day.

Day #46, 12/30/2010

Meditation: God's plan is better than anything you could possibly imagine.

Focus on the fact that God will provide you with everything that you need for each moment of your life. Let go of your ideas about what and how things should be, which would limit how fully God can bless you. If your head is full of your plans, it creates resistance for God to work His plans. Expect and accept that God will guide you, then appreciate and share all of God's blessings and His bounty.

Positive intention for the day: Constantly look for God's will. Work with God's plan for your life.

Day #47, 12/31/2010

Meditation: God is all that you need.

Clear the garbage out of your mind and your heart. Stay focused on God, knowing that God will always be all that you need. Good focus equals good motives and intentions. Good intentions equal good energy and good living.

Positive intention for the day: Fill with God's good energy, then project that out into other people's lives.

Day #48, 1/1/2011

Meditation: God is generous and loving. He wants to fill you with love and fill your life with blessings.

Your part is to seek God's will and to open your mind and heart to God—the source of all goodness and love. Also open your heart and your life to others, so you can share God's goodness.

God will always be sure that you stay filled with what He wants you to pass on to others.

Positive intention for the day: Keep the channel open to what God wants you to receive, and then pass on to others.

Day #49, 1/2/2011
Meditation: Slow down and enjoy life today.

Living today fully doesn't mean running around, stressing out, and trying to cram as much as you can into today. Living fully means savoring each moment, being more aware and more fully present. Often that means slowing down enough to enjoy the moment, while God works in your life, building His creation.

Positive intention for the day: Enjoy each moment fully, one moment at time. Be aware of God's energy and efforts to enrich your life. Receive God's blessings; trust in God's promises.

Day #50, 1/3/2011
Meditation: God is on your team. Everything that you do today, you are doing together with God.

Your "guide" is within you and is always present. You can trust your inner self to guide and nurture you. Self-care is part of God's will for your life. You and God are partners on the same team. The stronger you get, the stronger your team is. You are a channel for God's love. You need to keep the channel clear of anger, resentment, and fear—and nurture kindness, generosity, and love—so God's love can freely flow through you to others.

CATHY C.

Positive intention for the day: Goodness within creates goodness flowing out. Take good care of yourself so that God and you can work together to gift the universe.

Day #51, 1/4/2011
Meditation: Surrender to God's plan for your life.

If you let God control your life and your choices, you will see constant improvement. You will also notice a ripple effect of goodness entering into the lives of those close to you. Make it your goal to act as God's agent, to bring about whatever God wills, and to watch everything around you improve.

Positive intention for the day: Do your part, and then get out of the way.

Day #52, 1/5/2011
Meditation: Be a channel for God's love.

Free yourself of all anger, fear, and resentment, so God's love can freely flow from within your heart into the lives of others. God keeps planting seeds of love in your soul, but it's up to you to water the seedlings daily and to keep pulling the weeds that try to choke them out.

Positive intention for the day: Nurture what God has given you, and let the sunlight of the Spirit grow goodness within you today.

Day #53, 1/6/2011
Meditation: How can you serve God today?

In meditation, ask, "Where does God want me? How does God want me to treat others today? Who can I help today?" Life is a dance inspired by God's love. You can make the world more beautiful by simply expressing the joy you feel when you are connected to God. You can brighten someone's life by portraying the happiness that God has given you.

Positive intention for the day: Submit to God's lead in your dance through life today.

Day #54, 1/7/2011
Meditation: There is a lot of power in surrender!

So much power is available to you, if you let go and let God take control of your life. There is so much healing available from God, for you and for your relationships, if you do things God's way. There is so much happiness available in God's hands.

Positive intention for the day: Grab ahold of the blessings that God provides, on the path He has planned for you.

Day #55, 1/8/2011
Meditation: Serenity is rooted in faith, but you have to walk the steps from faith to serenity.

The Serenity Prayer talks about acceptance, courage, and wisdom. Faith gives you the courage to walk through difficult circumstances. Walking through difficulties provides you with wisdom gained from experience. Acquired wisdom gives you the ability to accept your circumstances.

Serenity is a process. You have to go through the steps of faith, courage, wisdom, and acceptance to get there. You can feel fear and faith at the same time, but through exercising courage, you can gain wisdom and then experience acceptance and serenity.

Positive intention for the day: Do the footwork to get from faith to serenity.

Day #56, 1/9/2011
Meditation: God will keep giving you opportunities to be of service to others.

Let down any defensive walls that keep you distant from others. Being responsible means being able to care enough about others to respond to their needs. That requires getting close to others. Make real connections.

Positive intention for the day: Go where God leads and offer your services, knowing that God will replenish your supplies and you will not become drained—if you stay in God's will.

Day #57, 1/10/2011
Meditation: God is everything or He is nothing.

Slow down. Avoid dashing through your day in a frenzied rush, trying to accomplish everything on your list of errands to do, etc. It is more meaningful to do little steps with great care and awareness. God's will can be accomplished in little actions; you don't need to make huge sacrifices or big donations to do God's will.

Positive intention for the day: Try to see God in all things and to do God's will throughout all of the little steps of your day.

Day #58, 1/11/2011
Meditation: The absence of bad is good.

Pause and recognize that when nothing bad is happening, the universe is being good to you. When that is the case, respond with good energy to sustain the flow of goodness. Promote goodness by first filling yourself with gratitude for how good you have it, then share that good feeling with others.

Positive intention for the day: Be aware of the magic and the miracle of everyday life.

Day #59, 1/12/2011
Meditation: You are never alone.

God brings other people to us—to sustain and support us, to celebrate life with us, and for us to love, cherish, and enjoy. Every time we connect with someone and recognize God's child within another person, we connect with God again.

Positive intention for the day: Be open to seeing God within everyone you meet, and connect with God as often as possible.

Day #60, 1/13/2011
Meditation: God is within you. You have access to God every minute of every day.

God's power, wisdom, and love are always there, waiting for you to stop scurrying around. All you need to do is pause and connect. What a joy, and what a miracle it is, that the

Creator of the universe really wants to have an intimate, profound relationship with each of us! Slow down and enjoy that connection. God speaks to us in the quiet times.

Positive intention for the day: Try to be fully present in your relationship with God.

Day #61, 1/14/2011
Meditation: God's power is available to us all, and it is only limited by our self-will.

We all have a need to exert control over our lives, but if we would totally "let go, let God," we would be capable of doing amazing, miraculous things.

When you pause and try to exercise God's will in a situation, you are accessing a power to accomplish much more than anything you could do by yourself. God wants you to be happy, joyous, and free. You should have no reservations on completely committing yourself to that plan for your day, one day at a time.

Positive intention for the day: Connect to the correct power source for today's activities.

Day #62, 1/15/2011
Meditation: We are empowered to create good when we connect with God and allow Him to direct our thoughts, feelings, and actions.

You can use God's love to create more love in your life. You can use God's goodness to create more goodness in this world. When you bring good energy into your interactions with people, your good energy can then be passed on from them to many others. Be aware that the energy we extend is like the ripples created by a rock dropped into a pond; our energy continues affecting others.

Positive intention for the day: Remove the "blocks" of your character defects (self-centeredness and selfishness) and eliminate the distractions of resentment, anger, and fear. Be prepared to bring good, clear energy to whatever God directs you to do. Be a tool in God's hands.

Day #63, 1/16/2011
Meditation: God nurtures you, protects you, and comforts you.

You can be a channel for God's love, comfort, and peace in this world. Think in terms of "us" all being connected, not in terms of "you" and "others," to help you be more open to freely sharing what God is giving you. Starve your ego by not feeding it with your attention. Try to stay focused on being part of God's family.

Positive intention for the day: Be more responsive when God nudges you to do His will.

Day #64, 1/17/2011
Meditation: Our actions and energy affect the universe.

Like tributaries of a river, the energy that we produce continues branching out and effecting others. Are you adding pollutants of negativity, or are you sending out love and creating beauty and goodness with what you are adding to this day?

Positive intention for the day: Be aware of the type of energy you allow to leave your person and saturate your surroundings.

Day #65, 1/18/2011
Meditation: Right now is glorious!

Take a moment to totally soak in the wonders of your present moment. Slow down and appreciate how good you have it. Fully experience your connection to God and all of His creations.

Positive intention for the day: Be aware of and grateful for all of your blessings.

Day #66, 1/19/2011
Meditation: We are all connected.

There is a piece of God inside all of us. Remember that when you interact with other people. The person you are irritated at for slowing down the checkout line is also a child of God.

Positive intention for the day: Feel the connections you have with everyone. Look for the similarities, and honor the divine within all.

Day #67, 1/20/2011
Meditation: How can you be of service today?

Try to let go of selfish, self-centered, and self-seeking thoughts about your issues (resentments, etc.), just for today. Look for opportunities to extend God's love and grace to others.

Positive intention for the day: Feel God's love, and experience the gift of serenity—then give it away.

Day #68, 1/21/2011
Meditation: God cares about how you feel.

God wants to meet your needs. God will help you walk through your day, and He'll help you deal with your feelings. God will help you carry those feelings that are too heavy for you to carry by yourself. You are never alone.

Positive intention for the day: Slow down, pay attention to how you feel, and then share your feelings with God. God cares about how you are feeling.

Day #69, 1/22/2011
Meditation: Expand your gratitude. Appreciate the commonplace things in your life for the gifts that they are.

The beauty, the magic, and the miracles of God's creation are beyond our ability to fully comprehend and appreciate. Stop to think what a blind person with restored vision would appreciate (probably a lot more that you do) looking at raindrops falling on leaves, tree branches swaying in the wind, etc. How much of the beauty of this day will you notice?

We should all see our relationships from a refreshed point of view also. Try to imagine how someone who has recently returned from years of solitary confinement would view your relationships—probably with great appreciation and gratitude rather than taking those relationships for granted.

Positive intention for the day: Try to see the world with new eyes. Savor all of your blessings, including the ones you have come to take for granted. You are as rich as you realize you are.

<u>Day #70, 1/23/2011</u>
Meditation: Appreciate fully each moment in time.

This exact moment is full of gifts and blessings. You grow by experiencing the lesson that exists in your current situation. You become better at living and loving, through experiencing and working with your present moment.

Positive intention for the day: Be more fully aware of everything that is going on right now. Life is a banquet; don't settle for nibbling on appetizers.

<u>Day #71, 1/24/2011</u>
Meditation: Ask how you can be a tool in God's hand today.

Set aside any need to control, as well as being judgmental, and simply try to extend God's love in all situations. Stop acting like you know better than God. God loves us all unconditionally. When you judge someone and you decide that person isn't "good" enough, you are trying to apply higher standards than God. Try to see the beautiful God's child in everyone.

Positive intention for the day: Fill with God's grace and love, then extend it to others.

<u>Day #72, 1/25/2011</u>
Meditation: Claim your identity as a child of God.

You are of value. You are a lovable, loved, and loving child of God. Wear that badge with pride. Everyone you meet should know by your attitude and your actions that you are a representative of God.

Positive intention for the day: Fill yourself with God's love and grace, so that you have what God wants you to share with others throughout your day.

Day #73, 1/26/2011
Meditation: Stay open and aware of the experiences God brings you.

Respond to others and to situations out of God's grace, with God's love. God's grace and love will expand, if focused on and cultivated.

Positive intention for the day: Stay connected to God and enjoy your connections with your fellows. Receive, as well as give, God's love.

Day #74, 1/27/2011
Meditation: We are all on a fabulous, exciting journey!

God will give you everything you need to have a great big beautiful day today. Open your mind and heart to being connected to God. Stay connected to God's energy and appreciate the blessings of this day.

Positive intention for the day: Savor the gifts of this day, and appreciate the love that surrounds you.

Day #75, 1/28/2011
Meditation: We are all connected, in the river of life.

We are all flowing through life together. We should move as harmoniously as possible through our days—without causing problems, irritations, and conflicts.

If you soak up God's love during meditation, that will create a buffer pad around you, so if you wind up in friction with others during your day, the grace of God will soften the impact for everyone.

Positive intention for the day: Blend with all others in today's journey. Don't cause waves and turbulence.

Day #76, 1/29/2011
Meditation: God showers you with blessings all of the time. You have a responsibility to pass them on.

If you don't nurture the blessings that God gives you, they can wither and die, instead of growing into something beautiful. The "pass it on" habit spreads the roots of your blessings and makes them stronger. Cultivate your gifts like a farmer tilling the soil and watering the seeds he has been given, so that beautiful plants can grow and benefit others.

Positive intention for the day: Be mindful of your blessings, and of your responsibility to nurture them and share them with others.

Day #77, 1/30/2011
Meditation: You have an appointment with life today—an assignment to live *today* as fully as possible.

You don't need to spend today stuck carrying around yesterday's baggage. God wants you to forgive the person you were and the mistakes you made getting to where you are today. We learn and grow when we correct the mistakes we make. Look for the lesson, without judging yourself. God wants you to enjoy living life as the person you are today. Start your day over with a clean slate.

Positive intention for the day: Be positively present in this exact moment, *now!*

Day #78, 1/31/2011
Meditation: Ask God to saturate and cleanse your mind and heart. Fill with love, compassion, and faith.

Everything is exactly the way it's supposed to be. You may not see the lesson or the purpose for a situation right now, but in hindsight, it often becomes clear that every step along the way was a necessary piece of God's plan. This exact step is necessary; you don't need to know why right now.

Positive intention for the day: Trust God, no matter what.

Day #79, 2/1/2011
Meditation: God is always with you, and He wants the best for you.

If you follow God's guiding hands today, you will have a smooth path. All you have to do is one "next indicated" step, one step at a time. That's all. God's love and grace will surround and sustain you. You will be given the strength, wisdom, and compassion to do today well. It will be much less stressful, if you focus on that fact that God is in charge.

Positive intention for the day: Relax and follow God's guidance today.

<u>Day #80, 2/2/2011</u>
Meditation: God loves you unconditionally. He is always patient, loving, tolerant, and kind.

Be thankful for God's ever-present, sustaining love. God is creating a tapestry out of the experiences of your life. It's all for a purpose. The dark spots have meaning and significance in the overall picture. Your part is to follow God's guidance, let Him love you, and enjoy His blessings. You need to remember that God is creating what He has planned for your life. He is creating the big picture, which you cannot see right now.

Positive intention for the day: Share God's blessings with others, expanding the beautiful tapestry of God's love in this world.

<u>Day #81, 2/3/2011</u>
Meditation: You have a blessed life!

Whenever you are tired or stressed, you can connect with God and recharge. You can rest in His strength and be comfortable and comforted. Everything you need will be given to you at the right time—in His time. Life is too short and too precious to waste being stressed and worried about possible problematic tomorrows.

Positive intention for the day: Relax and enjoy your day. Enjoy *now*.

<u>Day #82, 2/4/2011</u>
Meditation: We are on an incredible journey called life.

Sometimes the experiences we are walking through are breathtakingly beautiful, and sometimes we travel a rough stretch of road, but each step you take has a purpose. If you try to follow God's guidance and live God's will, things will get better.

Positive intention for the day: Enjoy the scenery as you travel on your life's journey. Fully embrace the experience you are having right now. Don't waste any precious moment, and remember that each moment is precious.

Day #83, 2/5/2011
Meditation: You are a human *being*, not a human doing.

You can slow down and accomplish everything you need to, without stressing yourself or the people around you with an agitated need to accomplish everything that you do to a really high standard. There will always be more tasks to accomplish as you continue on life's journey, but if you keep focusing on the steering wheel, you'll miss the beautiful scenery around you.

Positive intention for the day: Don't let the work that needs to be done today detract from the joy of your journey.

Day #84, 2/6/2011
Meditation: You are connected to everyone and everything in creation.

Look at the beautiful world in which we live, and realize that each of us also contains that same beauty. Feel the connection, and treat all created things with awe and respect. Think of today as a glorious tapestry of interwoven threads, and be thankful to be part of the combined beauty that we are all creating together.

Positive intention for the day: Be the most beautiful contribution you can be to the collective canvas of today's world.

Day #85, 2/7/2011
Meditation: When you align yourself with God's will, you have more to offer others.

As you work through the process of clearing away the wreckage of your past, you will become more capable of helping others. One of the reasons we do an inventory and discard baggage that is no longer useful is that we are more capable of helping others when we ourselves are unburdened.

Positive intention for the day: Clean house, soak up God's love and grace, and then share it with others.

Day #86, 2/8/2011
Meditation: You are right where you're supposed to be right now.

Everything you experience today is exactly the way it's supposed to be. Your part is to look for the lesson that is appearing in your life right now.

Positive intention for the day: Look for the lesson, deal with it, learn from it, and be a part of God's plan for today.

Day #87, 2/9/2011
Meditation: It's okay to rest and recharge.

If you take time to pause in your daily activities, and soak in God's love and grace, you will have the resources you need to be of service to others throughout your day.

Positive intention for the day: Be a part of the mighty river of God's love flowing through this world. God's power is always available to you. Relax and go with the flow.

Day #88, 2/10/2011
Meditation: When you are in prayer and meditation, God fills you, so you can give to others.

You can be a reflection of God's love and grace, if you spend time in stillness. You can reflect God, like the surface of a lake, only when your waters are smooth. When you are upset or agitated, you cannot create a good reflection of God. When you are calm, you can reflect God's love to others through your words and actions.

Positive intention for the day: Stay mindful of the need to set aside quiet times to connect with God. Bring that calmness and that connection into your present moments as much as possible, so you can reflect God into the world around you.

Day #89, 2/11/2011
Meditation: The more you meditate and connect with God, the more you become a part of His plan.

The more you focus on being a part of God's will, the more in harmony with all others you become, and the fewer conflicts and chaos there are in your life. God's will for your life is more harmony and less conflict.

Positive intention for the day: Stay focused on realizing God's will for your life.

Day #90, 2/12/2011
Meditation: There is meaning and purpose to everything.

You are part of, and interacting within, an amazing cosmos—an orchestration of miracles. Although you can't see or comprehend much of it, try to stay mindfully aware that everything is a significant part of the same magnificent creation. Respect the value of all others and of everything that God has created.

Positive intention for the day: Feel the joy of being part of God's plan, and try to interact smoothly with all of Creation.

———————————

To be continued, one day at a time.

BIBLIOGRAPHY

Alcoholics Anonymous, third edition. Alcoholics Anonymous World Services, Inc., 1976.

Tom R., *Prayer and Meditation: A Practical Guide to the Life Promised in Step 11*. Denver, CO: Practically Spiritual Books, 2013.

Twelve Steps and Twelve Traditions. Alcoholics Anonymous World Services, Inc., 1952.

ENDNOTES

1   *Alcoholics Anonymous*, 68.

2   *Alcoholics Anonymous*, 25.

3   *Twelve Steps and Twelve Traditions*, 101 (emphasis added).

4   *Alcoholics Anonymous*, 75.

5   *Alcoholics Anonymous*, 85 (emphasis added).

6   *Around the Year with Emmet Fox*, Jan. 9.

7   *Twelve Steps and Twelve Traditions*, 101 and 102.

8   *Alcoholics Anonymous*, 63.

9   *Alcoholics Anonymous*, 76.

10   *Alcoholics Anonymous*, 84.

11   *Alcoholics Anonymous*, 59.

12   *Alcoholics Anonymous*, 50.

13   *Alcoholics Anonymous*, 86 and 87.

14   *Twelve Steps and Twelve Traditions*, 97 and 98.

15   *Alcoholics Anonymous*, 546.

16   1*Twelve Steps and Twelve Traditions*, 98.

17   *Twelve Steps and Twelve Traditions*, 98.

18   *Alcoholics Anonymous*, 71.

19   *Twelve Steps and Twelve Traditions*, 101.